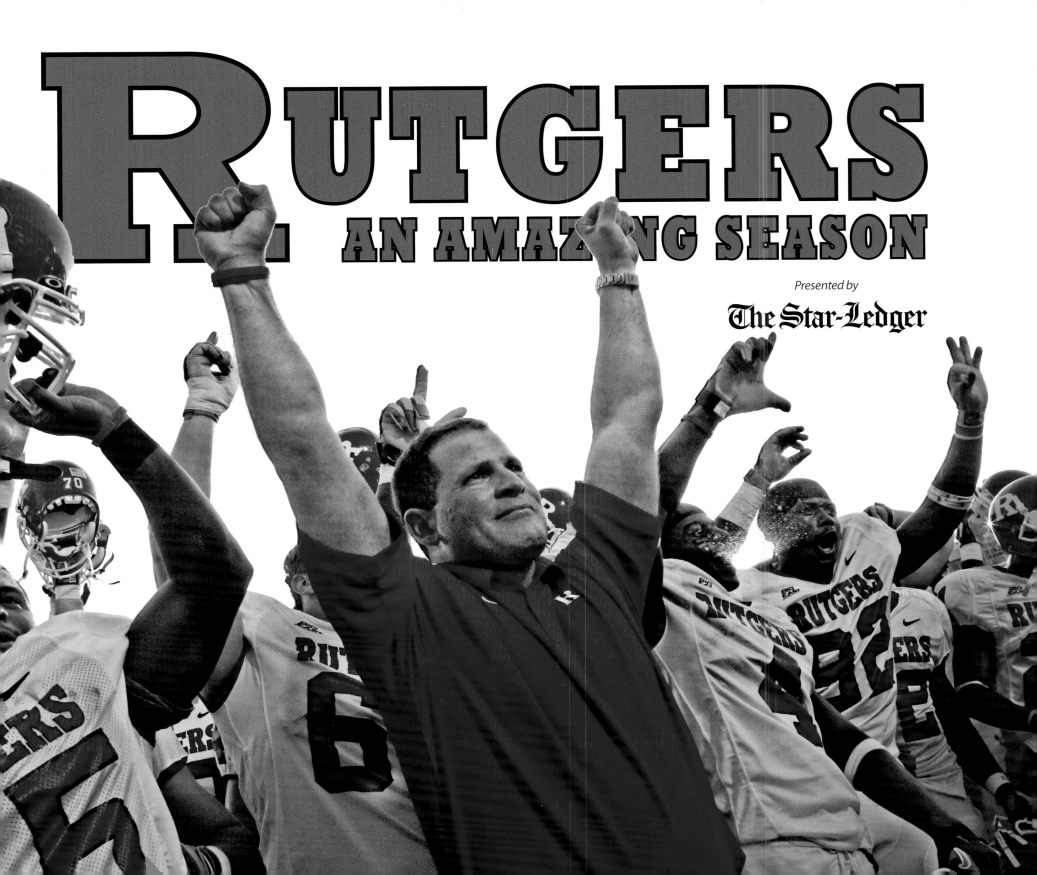

RUTGERS

AN AMAZING SEASON

Presented by

The Star-Ledger

Published by Pediment Publishing, a division of The Pediment Group, Inc. www.pediment.com Printed in Canada.

CONTENTS

You couldn't make this stuff up

It was a time of hope and a time of mystery. They knew the seasons of 1-11 and 2-9 were long gone. But they also knew they were carrying 137 years of Rutgers' football or about more than a century of pure 100-yard depression and pain on their backs that day in August.

As the Scarlet Knights assembled for the start of two-a-day practices, there was Ray Rice, coming off a 1,000-yard freshman season. There was Brian Leonard, who put honor and commitment above NFL money. There was placekicker Jeremy Ito, the one they called "the judge," and the precocious sophomore quarterback Mike Teel. There was the core of an improving defense and two-dozen seniors who had suffered through the lean years.

And striding across the field, bull horn at the ready, came the coach, Greg Schiano, the leader who had pulled Rutgers from the bottom of the Division 1-A world and marched to the school's first bowl game in 27 years.

Now, the Scarlet Knights were poised on a tightrope in a precarious balancing act. A fall would send them back where they came from. But the journey across it could cast them up into the stars.

Rutgers football fans, who had finally been given hope, held their breath and prayed for more.

What happened next is the stuff of legends. Rutgers blossomed into the Whirlwind of the Big East — a magnet for the oldest of the old guard and a student body that suddenly learned all the words to the alma mater, "On the Banks of the Old Raritan."

The season that began under a broiling summer sun would eventually become one for the history books:

- 11 victories
- A BCS ranking that soared as high as sixth
- A first-team All-America selection for defensive tackle Eric Foster
- Another 1,000-yard season for Rice and talk of a Heisman Trophy in 2007
- A National Scholar-Athlete Award for Leonard, who cemented his legacy as the greatest all-purpose player in Rutgers history
- National coach of the year awards for Schiano

You will find it all in these pages. The Texas Bowl blowout of Kansas State that was the first postseason victory for the school that started it all. Manny Collins' intercep-tion to preserve a victory over North Carolina. Ray Rice's 228-yard day against Pitt that included the longest run of his career (63 yards). The pain that followed the triple-over-time loss to the Mountaineers that cost the Scarlet Knights the Big East championship and kept them out of the Orange Bowl.

And then there's Louisville.

Ah, Louisville.

The night the old guard pulled its red sweaters out of mothballs and went up-stream, red team. Students who didn't even know where Rutgers Stadium was two years ago became an army — a loud army — to watch the Scarlet Knights play the third-ranked Cardinals. It was the night that best epitomizes what Schiano and Bob Mulcahy, the athletic director who took a chance on the young coach and never lost faith, did to make Rutgers the best damned college football story in America.

On that night, in front of a national cable television audience, the Scarlet Knights fell behind by 18 points only to claw their way back and tie the game in the fourth quarter. Then came a drive for the ages. Starting on their own 9-yard line, the game seemed headed for overtime until Teel and Leonard collaborated on a 26-yard pass and run. Then Rice broke free for 20 yards to set up field goal by the sure-footed Ito. Only, this time Ito missed. But wait! Louisville was off-sides. This time, with 13 seconds on the clock, he split the uprights.

And when it ended...

But why spoil it here.

Start turning the pages.

You couldn't make this stuff up.

Jerry Izenberg, sports columnist for The Star-Ledger

■ **Far left:** Head coach Greg Schiano watches practice from the stands on the first day of practice at Rutgers Stadium. *CHRIS FAYTOK PHOTO*

■ **Following page:** Fans storm the field after Rutgers defeats Louisville. *ANDREW MILLS PHOTO*

Rutgers beats North Carolina as Rice runs for 201 yards

By TOM LUICCI
STAR-LEDGER STAFF

CHAPEL HILL, N.C. — It turns out Rutgers had the right idea about launching the school's first official Heisman Trophy campaign this season. It just had the wrong player.

Know those video clips of Brian Leonard that run four times an hour in Times Square? Simply replace them with Ray Rice highlights.

That's essentially what the Knights did when North Carolina geared its defensive game plan to slowing down Leonard.

They called an audible in Rice.

They also issued a warning to all of their future opponents: You can stop one of their star running backs, but not both.

Rice, picking up where he left off after the greatest freshman rushing season in school history, ran for 201 yards and all three of Rutgers' touchdowns as the Knights opened with a 21-16 victory over North Carolina at Kenan Stadium — a result that sets up coach Greg Schiano's team nicely with three straight home games on tap.

But it wasn't until reserve defensive back Manny Collins picked off a Joe Dailey pass with the Tar Heels deep in Rutgers territory with 1:52 left that the Knights could finally exhale. Collins' second interception of the game enabled Rutgers to escape a second straight gut-wrenching loss in its opener. The Scarlet Knights squandered a 27-7 third-quarter lead in a 33-30 overtime loss at Illinois last year.

"I was getting real nervous there at the end," Leonard said.

That may have partly been due to the fact that he didn't have much else to do this day. Limited to six carries and four catches, the Heisman Trophy candidate saw Rice make the Tar Heels pay for their defensive strategy.

"Without a doubt, North Carolina dedicated resources to taking Brian Leonard out of the game," Schiano said. "That was clear by what they were doing defensively. That's okay. When you have more than one weapon like we do. ... That's what good teams do. If we can keep doing that, we'll be a good team."

"With both of us back there, it's like pick your poison," said Rice, who rushed for 1,120 yards last season. "I don't think you can stop both of us. One, maybe. But not both."

But Rice's efforts — he had a career-high 31 carries and scored on runs of 2, 7 and 10 yards — might have been wasted if Collins wasn't in the right place at the right time to cool off Dailey, who seemed to excel in Carolina's second-half switch to a hurry-up offense.

"This shows growth in our program," Schiano said. "Certainly you felt the momentum

■ **Far Right:** Ray Rice celebrates with wide receiver Shawn Tucker after scoring a touchdown in the first half.
NOAH K. MURRAY PHOTO

Right top: Tiquan Underwood beats North Carolina defender Chase Rice down the sideline for a first down during the first half. *NOAH K. MURRAY PHOTO*

Below right: Brian Leonard stretches for a first down during the first half. *NOAH K. MURRAY PHOTO*

Below: Mike Teel (14) takes one deep as Jeremy Zuttah (71) and Cameron Stephenson (63) protect their quarterback during the first half. *NOAH K. MURRAY PHOTO*

shifting in the fourth quarter. If you're going to be a winning football team, you need to make a play when that happens. Our kids did that. That's a tribute to them."

Dailey, who starred at St. Peter's Prep in Jersey City, was carving up Rutgers' defense in the second half, hitting 15 of his first 16 passes after halftime, as Carolina kept the Knights on their heels trying to protect a 21-10 third-quarter lead.

Collins' second interception off Dailey in the waning moments, this one at the Rutgers' 21-yard line, occurred just when it appeared the Tar Heels would rally for the victory.

"It feels good," said Collins, a fifth-year senior. "This is a little bit of a statement game for us."

Two series earlier, the defense came up big as well — with some help from instant replay. Rutgers had a 21-10 lead when Barrington Edwards ran 3 yards for what the officials ruled a touchdown. When a review showed Edwards didn't make the end zone, Carolina decided to try again on fourth-and-goal from the Rutgers' 1-yard line.

This time, middle linebacker Devraun Thompson collided with running back Ronnie McGill at the apex of both players' leap, forcing the ball loose. Rutgers' William Beckford recovered.

"I actually thought Dailey was going to go over the top," Thompson said. "It seemed like I was in the air forever."

Dailey (24-of-36 for 234 yards with one touchdown passing and one rushing) shook that off to drive the Tar Heels 89 yards on their next drive, getting to within 21-16 after the 2-point conversion pass failed with 5:09 to play. That was offset by his late interception.

"Very frustrating," said Dailey, who led Carolina to 403 yards of offense. ■

■ **Above right:** Wide receiver Dennis Campbell makes a catch during the second half. *NOAH K. MURRAY PHOTO*

■ **Right:** Ray Rice breaks away from North Carolina defenders in the first half. Rice ran for 201 yards in the game. *NOAH K. MURRAY PHOTO*

GAME ONE ~ SEPTEMBER 2, 2006

Right: Linebacker Devraun Thompson goes airborne but was called for roughing the passer after hitting North Carolina quarterback Joe Dailey in the second half.

NOAH K. MURRAY PHOTO

■ **Left:** Fans go wild at the end of the game after Rutgers wins its season opener. *NOAH K. MURRAY PHOTO*

■ **Below left:** Fans show their faith in the Scarlet Knights after their win in North Carolina.
NOAH K. MURRAY PHOTO

■ **Below:** North Carolina wide receiver Jesse Holley, a New Jersey native, looks at the scoreboard at the end of the game after Rutgers beat North Carolina 21-16.
NOAH K. MURRAY PHOTO

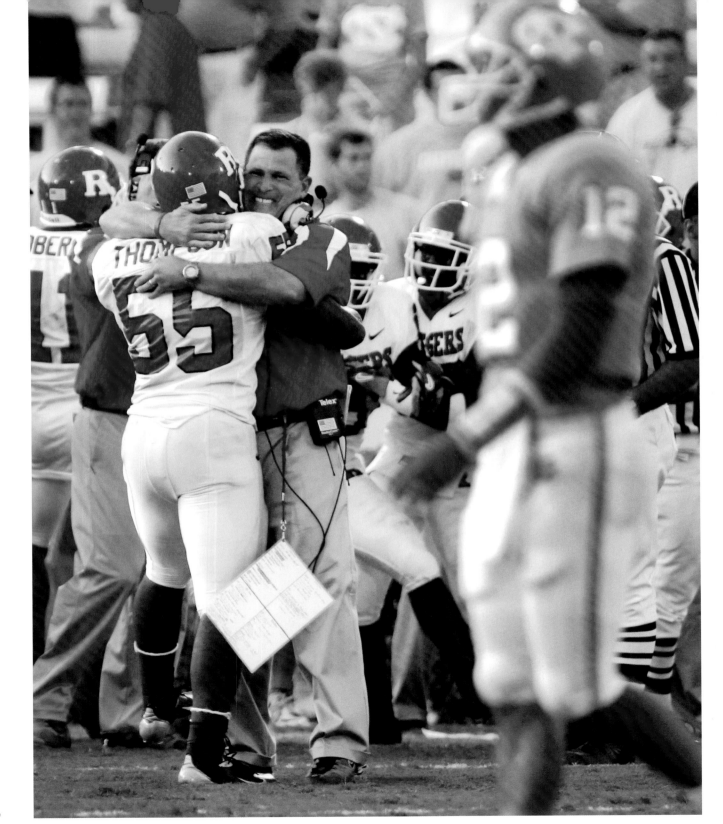

■ **Right:** Head Coach Greg Schiano hugs Devraun Thompson (55) as Rutgers beats North Carolina 21-16 in Chapel Hill, NC.

NOAH K. MURRAY PHOTO

■ **Far right:** Rutgers offensive Lineman Ryan Blaszczyk (61) celebrates with teammates as they walk off the field after beating North Carolina.

NOAH K. MURRAY PHOTO

Rutgers vs North Carolina
Sept. 02, 2006, at Chapel Hill, NC

Score by Quarters	1	2	3	4	Score	
Rutgers	7	7	7	0	21	Record: (1-0)
North Carolina	0	10	0	6	16	Record: (0-1)

Scoring Summary:
1st 02:32 RUTGERS - RICE, Ray 2 yd run (ITO, Jeremy kick), 12-93 5:33, RUTGERS 7 - NC 0
2nd 14:53 -NC - Dailey, J 4 yd run (Barth, C kick), 7-80 2:39, RUTGERS 7 - NC 7
  02:01 - RUTGERS - RICE, Ray 7 yd run (ITO, Jeremy kick), 8-63 4:11, RUTGERS 14 - NC 7
  0:00 - NC - Barth, C 47 yd field goal, 9-36 2:01, RUTGERS 14 - NC 10
3rd 03:50 - RUTGERS - RICE, Ray 10 yd run (ITO, Jeremy kick), 11-78 5:27, RUTGERS 21 - NC 10
4th 05:09 NC - Nicks, H 2 yd pass from Dailey, J (Dailey, J pass intcpt), 12-89 2:35, RUTGERS 21 - NC 16

Stats:

	RUTGERS	NC
FIRST DOWNS	22	25
RUSHES-YARDS (NET)	41-217	32-169
PASSING YDS (NET)	145	234
Passes Att-Comp-Int	20-14-0	36-24-2
TOTAL OFFENSE PLAYS-YARDS	61-362	68-403
Fumble Returns-Yards	1-14	1-19
Punt Returns-Yards	0-0	0-0
Kickoff Returns-Yards	3-44	3-87
Interception Returns-Yards	2-25	0-0
Punts (Number-Avg)	3-31.7	2-31.0
Fumbles-Lost	1-1	1-1
Penalties-Yards	7-41	8-60
Possession Time	33:24	26:36
Third-Down Conversions	8 of 13	8 of 13
Fourth-Down Conversions	0 of 0	0 of 1
Red-Zone Scores-Chances	3-4	2-3
Sacks By: Number-Yards	1-8	2-13

RUSHING: Rutgers-RICE, Ray 31-201; LEONARD, Brian 6-25; CAMPBELL, Denni 1-10; TEAM 1-minus 2; TEEL, Mike 2-minus 17. North Carolina-McGill, R 14-94; Dailey, J 8-38; Edwards, B 10-37.

PASSING: Rutgers-TEEL, Mike 14-20-0-145. North Carolina-Dailey, J 24-36-2-234.

RECEIVING: Rutgers-LEONARD, Brian 4-20; TUCKER, Shawn 3-46; CAMPBELL, Denni 3-38; RICE, Ray 2-13; HARRIS, Clark 1-16; UNDERWOOD, Tiqu 1-12. North Carolina-Foster, B 11-120; Nicks, H 7-63; Holley, J 3-25; Rome, B 1-11; Edwards, B 1-10; McGill, R 1-5.

INTERCEPTIONS: Rutgers-COLLINS, Manny 2-25. North Carolina-None.

FUMBLES: Rutgers-TEEL, Mike 1-1. North Carolina-McGILL, R 1-1.

SACKS (UA-A): Rutgers-GREENE, Courtne 1-0. North Carolina-Edwards, L 1-0; Taylor, H 1-0.

TACKLES (UA-A): Rutgers-GREENE, Courtne 6-2; ROBERSON, Derri 5-3; McCOURTY, Jason 6-0; GIRAULT, Ron 5-1; RENKART, Brando 4-2; FRIERSON, Quint 3-3; FOSTER, Eric 2-2; PORTER, Joe 3-0; McCourty, Devin 1-2; BECKFORD, Will 2-0;THOMPSON, Devra 0-2; MEEKINS, Ramel 0-2; JACKMAN, Leslie 1-0; TUCKER, Shawn 1-0; LEE, Glen 1-0; WESTERMAN, Jama 0-1; STAPLETON, Darn 0-1; MALAST, Kevin 0-1. North Carolina-Watkins, J 5-3; Walker, DJ 5-3; Edwards, L 5-2; Rice, C 5-2; Taylor, H 4-2; Taylor, K 3-1; Person, Q 3-0; Paschal, M 2-1; Guy, K 0-3; Rackley, B 0-3; Arnold, J 2-0; Balmer, K 2-0; Brown, M 1-1; Bynum, S 0-2; Mapp, D 0-2; Holley, J 1-0; Worsley, V 1-0; Wilson, EJ 1-0; Engram, D 1-0; Tate, B 1-0; Taylor, R 0-1.

Stadium: Kenan Stadium   **Attendance:** 50,000
Kickoff time: 3:36 PM   **End of Game:** 6:52 PM   **Total elapsed time:** 3:16
Officials: Referee: Gerard McGinn; Umpire: Mike Semcheski; Linesman: Matt Fitzgerald; Line judge: Tod Reese; Back judge: Ron Boyd; Field judge: Rich Street; Side judge: Greg Yette; Scorer: Steve Kirschner
Temperature: 81 F   **Wind:** W 8 mph   **Weather:** Sunny

■ **Left:** Greg Schiano celebrates with players at the end of the game after Rutgers beat North Carolina. *NOAH K. MURRAY PHOTO*

Rutgers defense settles the case

By **TOM LUICCI**
STAR-LEDGER STAFF

By the time Rutgers quarterback Mike Teel trotted onto the field for his second series, he was already working with a 14-0 lead — and neither he nor the Knights' offense had even managed a first down to that point.

"That's a pretty good feeling," Teel said.

As it turned out, it was one that never left.

Dominant defensively and able to come up with two big special-teams plays, Rutgers improved to 2-0 with a stunningly easy 33-0 rout of Illinois before a crowd of 41,036 at Rutgers Stadium, enabling the Knights to set their sights on the school's best start in a quarter century.

All it will take is beating Ohio U. at home this Saturday.

"It's a good start, but that's all it is — a start," said defensive tackle Eric Foster. "We still have a long way to go."

The most encouraging aspect of the Knights' latest victory is that they won easily despite an uneven performance by their offense. But their defense and special teams more than made up for it.

"To be a good football team you need to score in different ways," head coach Greg Schiano said. "We scored in all three phases, and that's what good teams do. I think we're getting better and closer."

This is how good the Knights were defensively: The only time Illinois crossed the 50 was to change sides of the field after the first and third quarters.

One week after rolling up 519 yards against 1-AA Eastern Illinois, the Illini (1-1) managed all of 126.

"The big thing to me is that we stayed focused throughout the game even with a big lead," safety Ron Girault said. "We never got complacent. Defensively, I think we felt like we had something to prove after (the North Carolina game). We weren't happy with the way we played in that one."

A school-record 78-yard punt by Joe Radigan started the rout, with the senior pinning Illinois on the 4-yard line for its first series. When three plays produced 3 yards for the Illini, Kyle Yelton's punt was blocked by Manny Collins and recovered in the end zone for a touchdown by Derrick Roberson, who said he also got a hand on the punt.

A series later, Rutgers had a 14-0 lead when Devin McCourty intercepted a Tim Brasic pass and returned it 38 yards — showing some of his old high school running back moves — for another score. That made it 14-0 after just 7:34 had elapsed and it wouldn't matter that the Knights offense managed a quiet 311 yards, that it wouldn't have a play longer than 27 yards and that it produced just two touchdowns, even though seven of the 11 drives started inside Illinois territory.

"The defense carried us today. That's a good feeling to know we can count on them," said sophomore tailback Ray Rice. "They know we'll be there for them too."

Rice had his fourth straight 100-yard game (finishing with 108 on 23 carries) and Teel was 14-of-24 for 145 yards with one touchdown pass and an interception. But the offense was out of sync all day, failing to produce any points on a first-and-goal from the 2-yard line in the second quarter and a first-and-goal from the 9 later in the game.

Teel did connect with tight end Clark Harris on a 1-

■ Far left: Defensive tackle Vantrise Studivant zeroes in on Illinois quarterback Juice Williams during the first half.
CHRIS FAYTOK PHOTO

yard TD pass to make it 20-0 (Jeremy Ito missed the extra point), with Rice scoring from a yard out and Ito converting a 37-yard field goal to make it 30-0 at the half. Ito's 39-yard third-quarter field goal produced the only points in the second half.

But none of it mattered because the Knights' defense recorded five sacks, pressured QBs Brasic and Juice Williams all game and held Illinois to 0-for-12 on third-down conversions.

This is also how good the defense was: ESPN2 cut away in the fourth quarter to show the end of the Akron-N.C. State game.

"This was exactly what we needed as a defense," said Foster, after the Illini managed 66 rushing yards on 29 attempts. "We know we can be a great defense that can carry this team if we need to. We just had to show it."

The feeble effort drew a curious response from Illinois head coach Ron Zook.

"Obviously, we stunk it up," he said. "That football team is good, but they're not 33 points better than us."

No, 50 may have been more like it — if the Knights' offense had delivered its 'A' game as well. ■

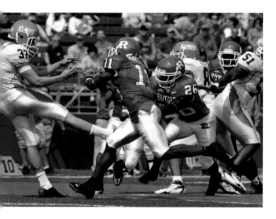

■ **Top:** Ray Rice and his teammates take to the field as their prepare to face the Illini. *CHRIS FAYTOK PHOTO*

■ **Above:** Derrick Roberson (11) and Manny Collins (26) block a punt by Illinois' Kyle Yelton in the first half. Roberson recovered the ball in the end zone for a touchdown. *CHRIS FAYTOK PHOTO*

■ **Right:** Joe Porter (24) knocks down Derrick Roberson (11) after Roberson recovered a blocked punt in the end zone for a touchdown during the first half. *CHRIS FAYTOK PHOTO*

■ **Left:** Defensive back Devin McCourty returns an interception for a touchdown in the first half.
CHRIS FAYTOK PHOTO

■ **Above:** Tight end Clark Harris fights for extra yards after a catch during the first half. *CHRIS FAYTOK PHOTO*

■ **Left:** Brian Leonard blows through a big hole in the Illinois defense in the first half. *CHRIS FAYTOK PHOTO*

■ **Right:** Greg Schiano congratulates Ramel Meekins during the first half of the game.

CHRIS FAYTOK PHOTO

■ **Far right:** Thanks to a block from tight end Clark Harris, Rutgers running back Ray Rice has a clear shot to the end zone in the first half.

CHRIS FAYTOK PHOTO

■ **Above:** Illinois' E.B. Halsey, of Elizabeth, has no room to run as he is hit by Rutgers' Damaso Munoz (17) and Joe Giacobbe (57) during the second half. *CHRIS FAYTOK PHOTO*

■ **Left:** Fans celebrate a touchdown during the first half by tossing one of their own into the air. *CHRIS FAYTOK PHOTO*

Illinois vs Rutgers

Sept. 09, 2006, at Piscataway, NJ

Score by Quarters	1	2	3	4	Score	
Illinois	0	0	0	0	0	Record: (1-1)
Rutgers	20	10	3	0	33	Record: (2-0)

Scoring Summary:

1st 10:39 RUTGERS - ROBERSON, Derri 0 yd blocked punt return (ITO, Jeremy kick), ILLINOIS 0 - RUTGERS 7

07:34 RUTGERS - McCourty, Devin 38 yd interception return (ITO, Jeremy kick), , ILLINOIS 0 - RUTGERS 14

02:09 RUTGERS - HARRIS, Clark 1 yd pass from TEEL, Mike (ITO, Jeremy kick failed), 6-62 3:01, ILLINOIS 0 - RUTGERS 20

2nd 09:08 RUTGERS - RICE, Ray 1 yd run (ITO, Jeremy kick), 7-47 3:46, ILLINOIS 0 - RUTGERS 27

00:34 RUTGERS - ITO, Jeremy 37 yd field goal, 8-35 1:13, ILLINOIS 0 - RUTGERS 30

3rd 07:51 RUTGERS - ITO, Jeremy 39 yd field goal, 6-24 2:31, ILLINOIS 0 - RUTGERS 33

Stats:

	ILLINOIS	RUTGERS
FIRST DOWNS	7	18
RUSHES-YARDS (NET)	29-66	40-166
PASSING YDS (NET)	60	145
Passes Att-Comp-Int.	21-7-2	25-14-1
TOTAL OFFENSE PLAYS-YARDS	50-126	65-311
Fumble Returns-Yards	0-0	0-0
Punt Returns-Yards	0-0	5-40
Kickoff Returns-Yards	3-49	0-0
Interception Returns-Yards	1-0	2-46
Punts (Number-Avg)	10-30.4	4-50.5
Fumbles-Lost	2-1	2-2
Penalties-Yards	9-65	5-30
Possession Time	26:59	33:01
Third-Down Conversions	0 of 12	6 of 13
Fourth-Down Conversions	0 of 0	0 of 1
Red-Zone Scores-Chances	0-0	3-6
Sacks By: Number-Yards	1-5	5-31

RUSHING: ILLINOIS-Thomas 7-38; R Mendenhall 2-22; Halsey 7-17; TEAM 1-0; Williams, I 7-minus 2; Brasic 5-minus 9. RUTGERS-RICE, Ray 23-108; YOUNG, Kordell 8-37; LOVELACE, Jabu 3-13; LEONARD, Brian 5-10; CAMPBELL, Denni 1-minus 2.

PASSING: ILLINOIS-Brasic 5-11-2-46; Williams, I 2-10-0-14. RUTGERS-TEEL, Mike 14-24-1-145; RICE, Ray 0-1-0-0.

RECEIVING: ILLINOIS-R Mendenhall 3-10; Warren 1-17; Cumberland 1-15; Ellis 1-12; Halsey 1-6. RUTGERS-LEONARD, Brian 5-42; HARRIS, Clark 4-47; UNDERWOOD, Tiqu 2-28; CAMPBELL, Denni 2-15; RICE, Ray 1-13.

INTERCEPTIONS: ILLINOIS-Ball 1-0. RUTGERS-McCourty, Devin 1-38; ROBERSON, Derri 1-8.

FUMBLES: ILLINOIS-TEAM 1-1; Brasic 1-0. RUTGERS-TEAM 1-1; RICE, Ray 1-1.

SACKS (UA-A): ILLINOIS-None. RUTGERS-WESTERMAN, Jama 2-1; FOSTER, Eric 1-1; FRIERSON, Quint 1-0.

TACKLES (UA-A): ILLINOIS-Leman 7-5; Steele 1-11; Mitchell 3-5; Ball 5-2; Harrison 3-3; Norwell 3-2; Thornhill 1-4; Lindquist 3-1; Miller 0-3; Norris 0-2; Walker 0-2; Davis, V 1-0; Carson III 1-0; Alaeze 1-0; Hoomanawanui 0-1; Sanders 0-1; Thomas 0-1; Maddox 0-1; Bellamy 0-1; Williams, S 0-1; Weil 0-1; Hudson 0-1. RUTGERS-THOMPSON, Devra 4-4; GREENE, Courtne 3-4; FRIERSON, Quint 3-2 GIRAULT, Ron 1-3; RENKART, Brando 0-4; WESTERMAN, Jama 2-1; FOSTER, Eric 1-2; BECKFORD, Will 0-3; MEEKINS, Ramel 0-3; ROBERSON, Derri 0-2; LEE, Glen 0-2; MALAST, Kevin 1-0; LEWIS, Chenry 1-0; WOOD, Brandon 1-0; STUDIVANT, Vant 1-0; COLLINS, Manny 0-1; MUNOZ, Damaso 0-1; TVERDOV, Peter 0-1; McCourty, Devin 0-1; GIACOBBE, Joe 0-1; QUAYE, Chris 0-1; LARYEA, Edmond 0-1; D'IMPERIO, Ryan 0-1; WATTS, Gary 0-1; KITCHEN, Zaire 0-1.

Stadium: Rutgers Stadium   Attendance: 41, 036

Kickoff time: 12:03 PM   End of Game: 2:57 PM   Total elapsed time: 2:54

Officials: Officials: Referee: S.Newman; Umpire: B.O'Hara; Linesman: M.Dolce; Line judge: D.Chesney; Back judge: D.Morris; Field judge: D.Swanson; Side judge: D.Leftwich; Scorer: Rutgers

Temperature: 77 F   Wind: calm   Weather: Hazy, mostly sunny

■ **Left:** Rutgers head coach Greg Schiano gives a thumbs up as he leads the team onto the field before the start of the game. *CHRIS FAYTOK PHOTO*

Defense, special teams bail out offense, prevent letdown

By TOM LUICCI
STAR-LEDGER STAFF

There was every chance for Rutgers to lay a New Hampshire-sized egg on the way to the school's best start in 25 years. But the Knights' defense and special teams wouldn't allow that to happen. Not this time.

This is how good those two units were: It didn't matter that quarterback Mike Teel threw three interceptions or that the offense produced just 17 points — none in the second half. Nor did it matter that Ohio started four drives in Rutgers territory.

Just as it did against Illinois a week earlier, the defense choked off the Bobcats at almost every turn after their first drive — even contributing a touchdown to the effort — as Rutgers improved to 3-0 with a 24-7 victory before a Homecoming crowd of 41,102 at Rutgers Stadium.

Pretty, it wasn't. But the Knights are off to their best three-game start since 1981 and look to be well on their way to 4-0 for the first time since 1980 with 1-AA Howard paying a visit on Saturday.

"The defense got us out of a lot of stuff," said tailback Ray Rice, who rushed for 190 yards and two touchdowns on 29 carries. "If the offense had a letdown, the defense and special teams were there to pick us up."

That didn't happen two years ago after Rutgers opened the season with the first signature victory of the Greg Schiano era by beating Michigan State. A week later, the Knights lost at home to 1-AA New Hampshire.

"I thought our guys did the things we had to do to win the football game," Schiano said. "We've gotten off to a fast start and it's very exciting, but we're still a work in progress."

Maybe not defensively. That unit answered any and all questions for the second straight week, holding Ohio (2-1) to 119 yards of total offense and to minus 6 yards rushing. The Bobcats scored on a 17-yard drive on their first possession after intercepting Teel for the first time, but couldn't add to their scoring total for the final 55 minutes and 23 seconds.

"You can be frustrated with the way you played, but you can't be frustrated with the outcome," said Teel, who finished 6-of-16 for 83 yards and now has just one touchdown pass and four interceptions this season. "You have days like this. The most important thing is to get the `W.'"

If there's a concern on this team after three games, it's the play of Teel, who still doesn't look comfortable — or confident. Schiano says the latter isn't an issue, but he did make a point of stopping by Teel's locker after the game.

"I said, `Good win.' He said, `Yeah, that's

■ **Far left:** Ohio's Tyler Russ discovers that tackling Ray Rice doesn't come without a price. *CHRIS FAYTOK PHOTO*

about all it is — a win,'" Schiano said. "I've been around a lot of quarterbacks who have had days like that."

The 17 points that Teel & Co. produced came off three drives that totaled 73 yards. The first touchdown, a 4-yard run by Rice midway through the first quarter, followed an interception by Ron Girault that allowed the offense to set up shop at the Ohio 31. Rutgers then added a 31-yard field goal by Jeremy Ito for a 10-7 lead early in the sec-

ond quarter after James Townsend forced Ohio punter Matt Lasher into a fumble off a low snap, with Kordell Young recovering. A shanked punt by Lasher later gave Rutgers the ball at the Bobcats' 38, where Teel engineered his longest drive of the game. It ended in four plays with another 4-yard touchdown run by Rice.

Then just before the half, Rutgers received a break and made the most of it when Ohio coach Frank Solich inexplicably called a pass on third

■ **Right:** A Rutgers fan rides the crowd in the first half after a Rutgers score. *CHRIS FAYTOK PHOTO*

■ **Below:** Devraun Thompson (55) sacks Ohio quarterback Brad Bower with help from Ramel Meekins (60) during the first half. *CHRIS FAYTOK PHOTO*

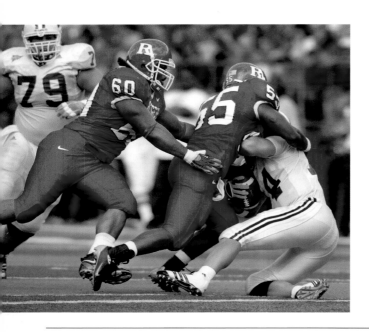

down with his team at its 5-yard line. Lineback-er Quintero Frierson hit quarterback Brad Bower and forced a fumble, with teammate Brandon Renkart recovering in the end zone for a Rut-gers touchdown just 46 seconds before the half. That made it 24-7 and that's how it stayed.

"We really found out a lot about our defense," said safety Courtney Greene, who rebuffed an Ohio drive with an end zone interception, the first of his career. "We got put in a lot of tough situations and we came through." ■

■ **Below:** Quarterback Mike Teel calls a play from under center in the first half. *CHRIS FAYTOK PHOTO*

■ **Sequence:** During the second half, Ohio's Michael Graham becomes the latest in a long line of defenders to get faked out by Brian Leonard's signature leap. *CHRIS FAYTOK PHOTOS*

■ **Above:** Brian Leonard spins past Ohio's Neil Jereb in the second half. *CHRIS FAYTOK PHOTO*

■ **Left:** Wide receiver Tiquan Underwood comes off the line against Ohio's Michael Hinton in the second half. *CHRIS FAYTOK PHOTO*

Ohio vs Rutgers
Sept. 16, 2006, at Piscataway, NJ

Score by Quarters	1	2	3	4	Score	
Ohio	7	0	0	0	7	Record: (2-1,1-0)
Rutgers	7	17	0	0	24	Record: (3-0)

Scoring Summary:
1st 10:23 OHIO - CHRISTY, Thomas 1 yd pass from EVERSON, Austen (LASHER, Matt kick), 6-17 3:25, OHIO 7 - RUTGERS 0

03:14 RUTGERS - RICE, Ray 4 yd run (ITO, Jeremy kick), 5-31 2:23, OHIO 7 - RUTGERS 7

2nd 14:49 RUTGERS - ITO, Jeremy 29 yd field goal, 4-4 1:29, OHIO 7 - RUTGERS 10

10:52 RUTGERS - RICE, Ray 4 yd run (ITO, Jeremy kick), 5-38 2:40, OHIO 7 - RUTGERS 17

00:46 RUTGERS - RENKART, Brando 0 yd fumble recovery (ITO, Jeremy kick), OHIO 7 - RUTGERS 24

Stats:

	OHIO	RUTGERS
FIRST DOWNS	8	13
RUSHES-YARDS (NET)	26-(minus) 6	38-217
PASSING YDS (NET)	125	83
Passes Att-Comp-Int	29-14-2	16-6-3
TOTAL OFFENSE PLAYS-YARDS	55-119	54-300
Fumble Returns-Yards	0-0	0-0
Punt Returns-Yards	3-90	1-(minus) 3
Kickoff Returns-Yards	3-46	2-30
Interception Returns-Yards	3-23	2-39
Punts (Number-Avg)	6-36.7	4-49.8
Fumbles-Lost	2-2	0-0
Penalties-Yards	9-55	2-30
Possession Time	30:08	29:52
Third-Down Conversions	5 of 16	4 of 11
Fourth-Down Conversions	0 of 1	0 of 0
Red-Zone Scores-Chances	1-3	3-5
Sacks By: Number-Yards	0-0	3-21

RUSHING: Ohio-McRAE, Kalvin 12-28; ABRAMS, Joshua 3-4; EVERSON, Austen 5-0; LASHER, Matt 1-minus 18; BOWER, Brad 5-minus 20. Rutgers-RICE, Ray 29-190; LEONARD, Brian 4-19; YOUNG, Kordell 2-11; TEEL, Mike 2-minus 1; TEAM 1-minus 2.

PASSING: Ohio-EVERSON, Austen 11-21-1-77; BOWER, Brad 3-8-1-48. Rutgers-TEEL, Mike 6-16-3-83.

RECEIVING: Ohio-NWOKOCHA, Chido 4-45; MAYLE, Scott 3-49; NORWOOD, W. 3-22; SYLVAN, Rudy 1-5; FITZGERALD, J. 1-3; CHRISTY, Thomas 1-1; McRAE, Kalvin 1-0. Rutgers-LEONARD, Brian 4-64; TUCKER, Shawn 1-11; HARRIS, Clark 1-8.

INTERCEPTIONS: Ohio-WRIGHT, T.J. 1-17; MUNCY, Matt 1-6; RUSS, Tyler 1-minus 2; KOENIG, Todd 0-2. Rutgers-GIRAULT, Ron 1-39; GREENE, Courtne 1-0.

FUMBLES: Ohio-EVERSON, Austen 1-1; LASHER, Matt 1-1. Rutgers-None.

SACKS (UA-A): Ohio-None. Rutgers-THOMPSON, Devra 2-0; FRIERSON, Quint 1-0.

TACKLES (UA-A): Ohio-RUSS, Tyler 8-5; MUNCY, Matt 4-3; WARD, Tony 4-3; MEYERS, Jordan 5-1; PARSON, Mark 3-1; GRAHAM, Michael 0-3; YATES, Shane 2-0; RENFRO, Lee 0-2; HINTON, Michael 1-0; MITCHELL, M. 1-0; SYKES, Brett 1-0; LAWRENCE, Idris 0-1; GOFF, Alan 0-1; LEUCK, Josh 0-1; HENLEY, Taj 0-1. Rutgers-FRIERSON, Quint 6-2; GREENE, Courtne 3-5; THOMPSON, Devra 3-4; FOSTER, Eric 2-3; RENKART, Brando 1-4; COLLINS, Manny 3-1; MEEKINS, Ramel 1-3; UNDERWOOD, Tiqu 2-0; GIRAULT, Ron 2-0; BECKFORD, Will 1-1; McCourty, Devin 0-2; ROBERSON, Derri 0-2; PORTER, Joe 1-0; D'IMPERIO, Ryan 1-0; YOUNG, Kordell 1-0; TOWNSEND, James 1-0; BELJOUR, Jean 1-0; LEONARD, Brian 1-0; TVERDOV, Peter 1-0; WOOD, Brandon 1-0; KITCHEN, Zaire 0-1.

Stadium: Rutgers Stadium   Attendance: 41,102
Kickoff time: 3:36 PM   End of Game: 6:29 PM   Total elapsed time: 2:53
Officials: Referee: J. McDaid; Umpire: G. Brenner; Linesman: T. Gray; Line judge: H. Campbell; Back judge: K. Washington; Field judge: R. Sokolowski; Side judge: B. Platt; Scorer: RUTGERS
Temperature: 77 F   Wind: NE 10 mph   Weather: Mostly cloudy

■ **Left:** Running back Ray Rice celebrates with the student section of the crowd after Rutgers beat Ohio 24-7. Rice ran for 190 yards in the game. CHRIS FAYTOK PHOTO

GAME FOUR ~ September 23, 2006

Rutgers enjoys a laugher ... but Teel isn't smiling

By TOM LUICCI
STAR-LEDGER STAFF

So, this is what $300,000 buys these days: The largest margin of victory in Greg Schiano's six years as head coach, the first 4-0 start since 1980 and a whole bunch of angst about quarterback Mike Teel and the passing game.

Rutgers thoroughly dominated undermanned Howard as expected, rolling to a 56-7 victory on the strength of seven rushing touchdowns before a crowd of 35,558 at Rutgers Stadium.

It was everything it needed to be for the Knights as they head into a three-game road stretch that starts Friday night with the Big East opener against South Florida.

Okay, everything except one thing: Teel's first big breakout game.

Schiano says he isn't worried about the third-year sophomore. Teel insists his confidence is fine. And his teammates genuinely seem to believe that when it comes to crunch time on the road, Teel will deliver.

He just hasn't come through in a big way yet, turning in another uneven performance against the 1-AA Bison, who happily

■ **Right:** Rutgers fans show their true colors as they cheer for the Scarlet Knights in the first half.
NOAH K. MURRAY PHOTO

■ Top right: After providing Rutgers with a comfortable lead, quarterback Mike Teel watches the game from the sideline. *MITSU YASUKAWA PHOTO*

■ Top left: Howard quarterback Martin Decembert (11) is swarmed by Rutgers defenders including Devin McCourty (21), Quintero Frierson (50), and Devraun Thompson (55) in the first half. *MITSU YASUKAWA PHOTO*

■ Below: Ray Rice of Rutgers breaks away from Howard's Rickey Jackson (17) in the first half. *NOAH K. MURRAY PHOTO*

fell to 0-3 thanks to the $300,000 guarantee that Rutgers will pay the school for the right to count a glorified scrimmage as its fourth game.

"You're going to go through adversity during a season. We trust in Mike," said sophomore tailback Ray Rice, who recorded his sixth straight 100-yard game — one shy of the school record — with 105 yards and three touchdowns on 23 carries. "If we need to win a game by passing, I know Mike is going to come

through. No question. I have faith in him. The whole team has faith in him."

At this point, it's not a faith supported by numbers. Teel finished 9-of-16 for 133 yards with one touchdown and another interception. It was his fourth straight passing game of 145 yards or less this year and in seven career starts (and 13 games overall) he has thrown for more than 200 yards just once.

He also has just four touchdown passes to

15 interceptions in his career.

"I haven't done it yet, so I can see why people are concerned," said Teel. "But as for me, personally? I'm not concerned at all. My confidence is fine."

Teel pointed to a career-long 45-yard touchdown pass to tight end Clark Harris as a sign of progress after a slow statistical start — although it really was an 8-yard pass that Harris ran 37 yards with.

"I was a lot happier with the way I played this game than last week (when he was 6-for-18 for 83 yards with three interceptions against Ohio)," Teel said. "We had a couple of deep shots. I missed the one to Shawn Tucker. We'll get that. I got the one to Clark.

"I think I'm doing all of the little stuff I need to do. I just haven't thrown for 300 yards yet."

Schiano, who is fully supportive of his quarterback, said Teel "got walloped" during an interception he threw just before the half, with Rutgers at the Howard 11.

So far, with a schedule that has consisted of North Carolina, Illinois and Ohio (who lost by a combined 107-20) and a 1-AA school, Teel hasn't been put in a position where he has had to win a game with his arm.

The running game churned out 215 yards against Howard, with Brian Leonard getting his first two touchdowns of the season, and the defense kept producing turnovers and choking off any hopes by the opposition (Howard's only score came on a 70-yard return of a Dimitri Linton fumble with 6:28 to play).

Rutgers' first four touchdown drives totaled 135 yards.

"The passing game isn't a concern for me. It will be there when we need it," said Harris. "If we can run the ball the way we have and win with defense, that's fine. We're 4-0. That's all that matters."

Actually, the passing game will matter at some point soon and probably in one of the upcoming road games.

"You win 56-7, we ran the ball effectively, how much do you have to throw?" said Schiano. "We're working on it in practice. We just have to do it a little more (in games)."

Rutgers did solve its problem of getting Leonard the ball. The fifth-year senior rushed for 62 yards on 10 carries and scored twice — the first two scores this year for the school's career touchdown leader with 42. He also caught three passes for 27 yards.

"It would have been nice for Mike to break out a little, too," said Leonard. "But I'm not worried about him. I've seen what he can do in practice." ■

■ **Below right:** Rutgers linebacker Kevin Malast tackles Howard quarterback Martin Decembert during the second half.
MITSU YASUKAWA PHOTO

■ **Below:** William Blanden of Howard is tackled by Derrick Roberson (11) and Ron Girault (43). *NOAH K. MURRAY PHOTO*

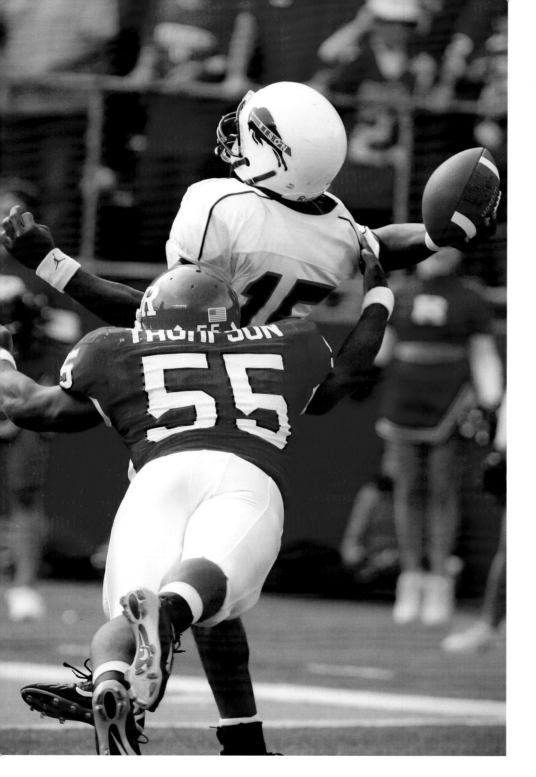

Howard vs Rutgers
Sept. 23, 2006, at Piscataway, NJ

Score by Quarters	1	2	3	4	Score	
Howard	0	0	0	7	7	Record: (0-3)
Rutgers	7	21	21	7	56	Record: (4-0)

Scoring Summary:

1st 10:13 **RUTGERS** - HARRIS, Clark 45 yd pass from TEEL, Mike (ITO, Jeremy kick), 3-53 1:06, HOW 0 - RUTGERS 7

2nd 14:50 **RUTGERS** - LEONARD, Brian 5 yd run (ITO, Jeremy kick), 4-17 1:47, HOW 0 - RUTGERS 14

08:45 **RUTGERS** - LEONARD, Brian 1 yd run (ITO, Jeremy kick), 4-12 1:44, HOW 0 - RUTGERS 21

04:36 **RUTGERS** - RICE, Ray 3 yd run (ITO, Jeremy kick), 6-53 2:39, HOW 0 - RUTGERS 28

3rd 11:40 **RUTGERS** - RICE, Ray 1 yd run (ITO, Jeremy kick), 8-66 3:20, HOW 0 - RUTGERS 35

08:02 **RUTGERS** - RICE, Ray 2 yd run (ITO, Jeremy kick), 5-30 2:21, HOW 0 - RUTGERS 42

02:26 **RUTGERS** - YOUNG, Kordell 2 yd run (ITO, Jeremy kick), 9-42 4:06, HOW 0 - RUTGERS 49

4th 11:47 **RUTGERS** - YOUNG, Kordell 1 yd run (ITO, Jeremy kick), 1-1 0:08, HOW 0 - RUTGERS 56

06:28 **HOWARD** - CLAIBORN, Thomas 70 yd fumble recovery (WIEHBERG, Dennis kick), HOW 7 - RUTGERS 56

Stats:

	HOWARD	RUTGERS
FIRST DOWNS	10	19
RUSHES-YARDS (NET)	31-48	53-215
PASSING YDS (NET)	124	142
Passes Att-Comp-Int	26-12-1	17-10-1
TOTAL OFFENSE PLAYS-YARDS	57-172	70-357
Fumble Returns-Yards	1-70	1-10
Punt Returns-Yards	4-29	1-28
Kickoff Returns-Yards	4-59	0-0
Interception Returns-Yards	1-16	1-0
Punts (Number-Avg)	9-31.2	5-52.8
Fumbles-Lost	2-2	1-1
Penalties-Yards	11-83	7-65
Possession Time	27:36	32:24
Third-Down Conversions	2 of 14	6 of 13
Fourth-Down Conversions	1 of 2	1 of 1
Red-Zone Scores-Chances	2-16	1-5
Sacks By: Number-Yards	1-5	5-29

RUSHING: Howard-BLANDEN,William 6-57; GARNER,John 1-29; RUTHERFORD,A. 4-7; COLEMAN,Keon 6-4; HAIGLER,Floyd 1-3; TURNER,Darrell 1-0; WHITTAKER,K. 2-minus 1; CORNIFFE,Martin 2-minus 1; JOHNSON,Brian 3-minus 4; DECEMBERT,M. 4-minus 12; TEAM 1-minus 34. Rutgers-RICE, Ray 23-105; LEONARD, Brian 10-62; CORCORAN, Jack 4-30; YOUNG, Kordell 7-20; LINTON, Dimitri 2-3; LOVELACE, Jabu 6-2; TEEL, Mike 1-minus 7.

PASSING: Howard-BLANDEN,William 5-11-0-42; TURNER,Darrell 5-6-0-54; DECEMBERT,M. 1-6-1-8; HAIGLER,Floyd 1-3-0-20; JOHNSON,Brian 0-0-0-0. Rutgers-TEEL, Mike 9-16-1-133; LOVELACE, Jabu 1-1-0-9.

RECEIVING: Howard-DUNCAN,Larry 2-37; SLAPPY,Rodney 2-20; HOOD,Arlandus 2-8; HELLAMS, L. 1-19; WHITTAKER,K. 1-14; ALEXANDER,U. 1-9; PERRY,Terry 1-8; CORNIFFE,Martin 1-6; GARNER,John 1-3. Rutgers-LEONARD, Brian 3-27; HARRIS, Clark 2-55; TUCKER, Shawn 2-31; CAMPBELL, Denni 2-20; BROWN, Tim 1-9.

INTERCEPTIONS: Howard-JACKSON,Rickey 1-16. Rutgers-GREENE, Courtne 1-0.

FUMBLES: Howard-COLEMAN,Keon 1-1; MOORE,Leonard 1-1. Rutgers LINTON,Dimitri 1-1.

SACKS (UA-A): Howard-JAMISON,Arando 2-0. Rutgers-LEWIS, Chenry 1-0.

TACKLES (UA-A): Howard-LOCKETT,Timothy 7-7; DOWDY,Robert 5-6; MEANS,Randell 3-7; CLAIBORN,Thomas 6-3; PEARCE,Danual 4-2; PINER,Edwin 2-3; JACKSON,Rickey 1-4; POPE,Geoffrey 2-1; ROBINSON,James 1-2; JAMISON,Arando 2-0; HARDIE,Rudolph 1-1; HELLAMS, L. 1-0; ALLEYENE,C. 0-1; CHANEY,Wilbur 0-1; WOOTEN,Marvin 0-1; CARTER,James 0-1. Rutgers-WATTS,Gary 3-3; BECKFORD,Will 2-3; FOSTER,Eric 1-4; MUNOZ, Damaso 2-2;McCourty,Devin 2-2; MALAST,Kevin 1-3; WESTERMAN,Jama 2-1; KITCHEN,Zaire 2-1; LEWIS,Chenry 1-2; THOMPSON,Devra 1-2; RENKART,Brando 1-2; GREENE,Courtne 2-0; PORTER,Joe 1-1; BINES,Blair 1-1; GIACOBBE,Joe 0-2; BAHAM,Robert 0-2; STUDIVANT,Vant 1-0; BELJOUR,Jean 1-0; McCOURTY,Jason 1-0; COLLINS,Manny 1-0; ANDERSON,Billy 1-0; LEONARD,Brian 1-0; FRIERSON,Quint 0-1; PIERRE-ETIE, J 0-1; QUAYE,Chris 0-1; TVERDOV,Peter 0-1; GIRAULT,Ron 0-1; MEEKINS,Ramel 0-1; ROBERSON,Derri 0-1.

Stadium: Rutgers Stadium **Attendance:** 35,558
Kickoff time: 2:08 PM **End of Game:** 5:23 PM **Total elapsed time:** 3:15
Officials: Officials: Referee: Jeff Maconaghy; Umpire: Bruce Palmer; Linesman: Tommy Walsh; Line judge: John Salmon; Back judge: Mark McAnaney; Field judge: Keith Parham; Side judge: James Brennan; Scorer: RUTGERS
Temperature: 70 F **Wind:** calm **Weather:** Overcast

■ **Above:** Devraun Thompson (55) sacks Howard quarterback William Blanden (15).

MITSU YASUKAWA PHOTO

Rutgers cooking with Rice

Super tailback rushes for 202 yards as Knights hold on to move to 5-0

By **TOM LUICCI**
STAR-LEDGER STAFF

TAMPA — Maybe it's just going to be like this all season for Rutgers, where nothing is ever easy.

But then, winning isn't supposed to be.

This time it took a pass breakup of a 2-point conversion try by cornerback Jason McCourty with 15 seconds to play, but the Knights found another way to win, holding on for a 22-20 victory over South Florida in the Big East opener for both schools at Raymond James Stadium.

In improving to 5-0 for the first time since 1976, Rutgers relied on the same formula it has all season, the same formula that had the Knights ranked No. 23 in both polls. They played tough, gritty, clutch defense and served up large helpings of Ray Rice.

Then they made Jeremy Ito's career-best 53-yard field goal stand up — but just barely.

"You've got to give credit to South Florida. They didn't give up," said Rice, who churned out 202 yards and two touchdowns on a career-high 35 carries. "They were the best team we played by far. It was scary to watch (at the end) but it's good for our defense to know they can come through."

With South Florida quarterback Matt Grothe able to drive his team 66 yards in eight plays without the benefit of a timeout, the Bulls (3-2) were within 22-20 when Grothe found Ean Randolph for a 16-yard touchdown pass with 15 seconds left.

On the 2-point conversion try, Grothe thought he had Amp Hill in the right corner of the end zone to force overtime, only to see McCourty break up the pass at the last instant.

"I just tried to get the ball out," said McCourty, a sophomore in his first year starting. "I think he might have caught it. I think I might have knocked the ball loose.

"All I know is I saw the ball on the ground and was looking for someone to hug."

Despite Rice's seventh straight 100-yard game — tying J.J. Jennings' 33-year-old school record — Rutgers had to earn everything it got because of the ongoing struggles of quarterback Mike Teel and everyone on the offense without the surname of Rice.

Teel finished 11-of-20 for a meager 100 yards with no touchdown passes and another interception (his sixth this year), and

■ Far right: Tight end Clark Harris celebrates after Rutgers beat South Florida 22-20. *CHRIS FAYTOK PHOTO*

didn't do much after engineering a 79-yard touchdown drive on Rutgers' first possession.

But Rutgers rallied from a 14-10 halftime deficit after USF rallied from a 10-0 first-half deficit thanks to Grothe. In the final 4:40 of the first half he drove the Bulls 80 yards and 70 for touchdowns, capping off both with scoring runs.

Rutgers' defense then came up with three second-half turnovers, with third-quarter interceptions by Courtney Greene and Ron Girault eventually getting the Knights the lead back.

Greene's pick resulted in a 40-yard field goal by Ito to make it 14-13 and Girault's gave Rutgers the ball at the South Florida 31-yard line. Rice capped off that all-running seven-play drive with a 7-yard TD run. That gave Rutgers a 19-14 lead with 13:04 left, which is where it stayed when the 2-point conversion pass failed.

Ito's 53-yard field goal with 7:02 to play padded the lead to 22-14 before linebacker Brandon Renkart seemed to dash the Bulls' last serious comeback hope. He stripped the ball from Grothe and recovered the forced fumble with USF at the Rutgers' 25-yard line.

But the Bulls had life again when Ito's 42-yard field-goal try was blocked with 2:32 to play.

That's when Grothe (16-of-25 for 241 yards, one TD, two INTs; 70 rushing yards and two scores on 14 carries) tried for more late-game heroics. Aided by two costly Rutgers penalties (of the season-high 11 committed by the Knights), he had the Bulls within two on his touchdown pass to Randolph.

And that's when McCourty saved the game by jarring the ball loose.

"That's just him busting his rear end off," Rutgers coach Greg Schiano said. "That's what our football team is — a bunch of fighters." ∎

■ **Right:** Head coach Greg Schiano stares down his team before leading them onto the field before the start of the game. *CHRIS FAYTOK PHOTO*

Right: Safety Ron Girault makes a tackle on South Florida's Colby Erskin in the first half. *CHRIS FAYTOK PHOTO*

Far right: South Florida receiver Amp Hill makes sure defensive back Manny Collins does not intercept a pass in the second half. *CHRIS FAYTOK PHOTO*

Below: Ron Girault (43) dives over Manny Collins (26) to take down South Florida wide receiver Amarri Jackson in the first half. *CHRIS FAYTOK PHOTO*

■ Above: Kicker Jeremy Ito celebrates his 53-yard field goal in the fourth quarter. *CHRIS FAYTOK PHOTO*

■ Above right: Greg Schiano yells for, and gets, an intentional grounding call on South Florida in the second half. *CHRIS FAYTOK PHOTO*

■ Right: Courtney Greene (36) celebrates his third-quarter interception against South Florida. *CHRIS FAYTOK PHOTO*

■ Far right: Running back Ray Rice gets past South Florida's Trae Williams to score on a 7-yard run in the fourth quarter to put Rutgers ahead for good. *CHRIS FAYTOK PHOTO*

Rutgers vs South Florida

Sept. 29, 2006, at Tampa, FL

Score by Quarters	1	2	3	4	Score	
Rutgers	7	3	3	9	22	Record: (5-0,1-0)
USF	0	14	0	6	20	Record: (3-2,0-1)

Scoring Summary:

1st 07:46 **RUTGERS** - RICE, Ray 3 yd run (ITO, Jeremy kick), 12-79 7:14, RUTGERS 7 - USF 0

2nd 06:35 **RUTGERS** - ITO, Jeremy 32 yd field goal, 7-11 3:44, RUTGERS 10 - USF 0

  04:40 **USF** - GROTHE, Matt 1 yd run (BENZER, Mike kick), 5-80 2:05, RUTGERS 10 - USF 7

  02:27 **USF** - GROTHE, Matt 22 yd run (BENZER, Mike kick), 5-70 1:40, RUTGERS 10 - USF 14

3rd 08:30 **RUTGERS** - ITO, Jeremy 40 yd field goal, 8-39 3:42, RUTGERS 13 - USF 14

4th 13:04 **RUTGERS** - RICE, Ray 7 yd run (TEEL, Mike pass failed), 7-31 3:57, RUTGERS 19 - USF 14

  07:02 **RUTGERS** - ITO, Jeremy 53 yd field goal, 7-8 4:29, RUTGERS 22 - USF 14

  00:15 **USF** - RANDOLPH, Ean 16 yd pass from GROTHE, Matt (GROTHE, Matt pass failed), 8-66 2:17, RUTGERS 22 - USF 20

Stats:

	RUTGERS	USF
FIRST DOWNS	19	19
RUSHES-YARDS (NET)	45-226	25-92
PASSING YDS (NET)	100	255
Passes Att-Comp-Int	20-11-1	26-17-2
TOTAL OFFENSE PLAYS-YARDS	65-326	51-347
Fumble Returns-Yards	0-0	0-0
Punt Returns-Yards	0-0	2-26
Kickoff Returns-Yards	2-44	1-20
Interception Returns-Yards	2-25	1-0
Punts (Number-Avg)	3-44.7	4-35.5
Fumbles-Lost	0-0	1-1
Penalties-Yards	11-91	7-56
Possession Time	37:16	22:44
Third-Down Conversions	6 of 13	4 of 9
Fourth-Down Conversions	0 of 0	0 of 0
Red-Zone Scores-Chances	4-4	2-2
Sacks By: Number-Yards	2-9	1-8

RUSHING: RUTGERS-RICE, Ray 35-202; LEONARD, Brian 8-30; TEEL, Mike 2-minus 6. USF-GROTHE, Matt 14-61; WILLIAMS, B. 9-18; RANDOLPH, Ean 1-11; ERSKIN, Colby 1-2.

PASSING: RUTGERS-TEEL, Mike 11-20-1-100. USF-GROTHE, Matt 16-25-2-241; GREEN, S.J. 1-1-0-14.

RECEIVING: RUTGERS-CAMPBELL, Denni 4-48; LEONARD, Brian 3-16; UNDERWOOD, Tiqu 2-24; HARRIS, Clark 1-10; BROWN, Tim 1-2. USF-RANDOLPH, Ean 6-49; JACKSON, Amarri 3-83; EDWARDS, Marcus 2-34; JOHNSON, Taurus 1-32; ERSKIN, Colby 1-22; GROTHE, Matt 1-14; BLEAKLEY, Will 1-11; GREEN, S.J. 1-8; GORDON, Devin 1-2.

INTERCEPTIONS: RUTGERS-GIRAULT, Ron 1-25; GREENE, Courtne 1-0. USF-WILLIAMS, Trae 1-0.

FUMBLES: RUTGERS-None. USF-GROTHE, Matt 1-1.

SACKS (UA-A): RUTGERS-MEEKINS, Ramel 1-0; BECKFORD, Will 1-0. USF-ST. LOUIS, Pat 1-0.

TACKLES (UA-A): RUTGERS-FRIERSON, Quint 5-0; GREENE, Courtne 4-1; GIRAULT, Ron 4-1; THOMPSON, Devra 3-1; McCourty, Devin 3-0; RENKART, Brando 3-0; BECKFORD, Will 3-0; MEEKINS, Ramel 3-0; FOSTER, Eric 2-1; ROBERSON, Derri 2-0; COLLINS, Manny 2-0; LEWIS, Chenry 1-0; HARRIS, Clark 1-0; STUDIVANT, Vant 1-0; KITCHEN, Zaire 1-0; WESTERMAN, Jama 1-0; JOHNSON, Sam 0-1; BAYOH, Sorie 0-1; TRACEY, Brian 0-1; WOOD, Brandon 0-1. USF-BURNETT, Jeremy 6-3; MOFFITT, Ben 6-2; ST. LOUIS, Pat 3-5; NICHOLAS, S. 7-0; VERPAELE, Danny 3-2; WILLIAMS, Trae 4-0; CRAY, Allen 4-0; BUIE, Jarriett 3-1; SELVIE, George 2-1; JENKINS, Mike 2-1; WILLIAMS, C. 1-0; MURPHY, Jerome 1-0; WILLIAMS, B. 1-0; HESS, Houston 1-0; GILLIAM, Ryan 1-0; GEORGE, Woody 1-0; GACHETTE, Louis 0-1.

Stadium: Raymond James   **Attendance:** 32,493
Kickoff time: 8:06 PM   **End of Game:** 11:20 PM   **Total elapsed time:** 3:14
Officials: Referee: Tom Tomczyk; Umpire: Rick Feeney; Linesman: Kavin McGrath; Line judge: Wayne Mackie; Back judge: Paul Vargo; Field judge: Dyrol Prioleau; Side judge: Bruce Williams; Scorer: Joe Kijanski
Temperature: 84 F   **Wind:** NW 8 mph   **Weather:** Partly Cloudy

■ **Left:** Rutgers players celebrate after beating South Florida, 22-20, improving their record to 5-0. *CHRIS FAYTOK PHOTO*

Teel looks like he's the real deal

By TOM LUICCI
STAR-LEDGER STAFF

ANNAPOLIS, Md. — Mike Teel kept insisting he didn't need the confidence boost, even as the whispers seemed to grow with each Rutgers victory and every uninspiring performance by its quarterback.

He was managing the offense the way the coaches wanted him to, he kept saying. He was making the right checks, playing within himself, allowing the Knights to ride the strength of running back Ray Rice's dazzling start.

His demeanor wasn't any different after the best game of his career helped No. 24-ranked Rutgers improve to 6-0 with a dominant 34-0 rout of Navy at Navy-Marines Corps Stadium, but his teammates sensed that his contributions meant a lot to the third-year sophomore.

"I don't want to put words in his mouth, but this game has to help him," star running back Brian Leonard said. "Every good game you have, it helps."

Especially if it's your first one.

The biggest question — the only one really — hanging over Rutgers during the school's best start in 30 years was answered in part this game.

The question: How would Rutgers' offense react when an opposing defense took away its power running game and kept Rice in check, as Navy did by limiting the nation's No. 2 rusher to 93 yards on 21 carries? The answer: career-highs of 215 passing yards and three TDs on 15-for-26 passing by Teel.

"It's his best game so far, but I don't think it's close to what his best game will be," tight end Clark Harris said. "He has a lot of big games left in that arm."

Teel viewed his near-breakout performance with the same detached, clinical view he had of his first five games, when Rutgers seemed to win almost despite him. The Knights came into the game ranked 112th nationally in passing, with Teel having thrown just two touchdown passes.

"I just went out and played the game and took what they gave me," he said. "Guys stepped up and made some plays."

Rutgers' defense did the rest, although it really wasn't a fair fight after Navy quarterback Brian Hampton — the team's rushing, passing and scoring leader — was carted off the field after suffering a dislocated left knee with 5:41 left in the first quarter.

Minus the leader of their triple option and forced to turn to seldom-used sophomore Kaipo Kaheaku-Enhada, the Mids never had a chance.

The nation's No. 1 rushing offense coming in (at 350.5 yards per game) was held to 113 yards on 50 carries as Navy was both shut out for the first time and held to its lowest offensive total (161 yards) in four years.

The Midshipmen also suffered seven sacks and were forced to punt 11 times.

"I think it definitely took something out of them when they lost their quarterback," defensive end William Beckford said. "But we also played great defense. Everyone took care of their responsibility and executed."

Navy coach Paul Johnson, while crediting Rutgers' defense, said the loss of Hampton was a huge emotional blow for his team, which fell to 5-2.

"A lot of guys had tears in their eyes (after Brian was hurt). It really affected some of them," he said. "But adversity happens and you have to go on and play."

Rutgers also made its own breaks after struggling to a

■ **Far left:** Rutgers defenders swarm Navy splitback Zerbin Singleton and stop him for no gain on the play.

FRANK H. CONLON PHOTO

10-0 halftime lead. The Knights broke open the game by blocking two third-quarter punts. The first, blocked by Manny Collins and recovered by Tim Brown at the Navy 23, resulted in a short touchdown drive that ended with a 9-yard scoring pass from Teel to Tiquan Underwood.

The second, blocked and recovered by Glen Lee, led to a field goal and a 20-0 lead. Underwood wound up with two TD catches and fellow wide receiver James Townsend stepped up with three receptions, highlighted by a 30-yard touchdown catch.

That was needed on a day Rice saw his streak of 100-yard rushing games snapped at seven.

"They wanted to stop the run and make us beat them with the pass," Rice said. "I'm really happy for Mike with the game he had." ■

■ **Left:** Wide receiver Tiquan Underwood scores a touchdown in the final minutes of the first half on a 25-yard catch. *FRANK H. CONLON PHOTO*

■ **Far left:** Tiquan Underwood (7) celebrates one of his two touchdown receptions with teammate James Townsend (83). Townsend also caught a touchdown pass during the game. *FRANK H. CONLON PHOTO*

Above: Freshman running back Kordell Young (8) breaks upfield on a run. Late in the game Young scored his third touchdown of the season.

FRANK H. CONLON PHOTO

Above right: Fullback Brian Leonard straight arms Navy linebacker Irv Spencer as he tries for extra yards.

FRANK H. CONLON PHOTO

Right: Rutgers defensive end Jamaal Westerman celebrates with head coach Greg Schiano. Rutgers beat Navy 34-0.

FRANK H. CONLON PHOTO

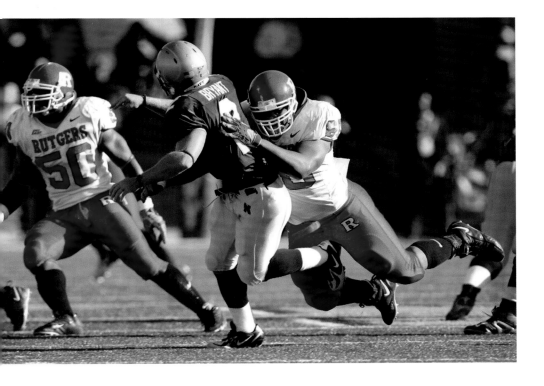

#24 Rutgers vs Navy
Oct. 14, 2006, at Annapolis, MD

Score by Quarters	1	2	3	4	Score	
Rutgers	0	10	10	14	34	Record: (6-0)
Navy	0	0	0	0	0	Record: (5-2)

Scoring Summary:

2nd 08:39 RUTGERS - ITO, Jeremy 30 yd field goal, 10-59 4:18, RUTGERS 3 - NAVY 0

01:17 RUTGERS - UNDERWOOD, Tiqu 25 yd pass from TEEL, Mike (ITO, Jeremy kick), 6-59 0:38, RUTGERS 10 - NAVY 0

3rd 09:21 RUTGERS - UNDERWOOD, Tiqu 9 yd pass from TEEL, Mike (ITO, Jeremy kick), 5-23 1:41, RUTGERS 17 - NAVY 0

05:59 RUTGERS- ITO, Jeremy 24 yd field goal, 4-3 1:42, RUTGERS 20 - NAVY 0

4th 13:23 RUTGERS - TOWNSEND, James 30 yd pass from TEEL, Mike (ITO, Jeremy kick), 6-54 2:29, RUTGERS 27 - NAVY 0

02:37 RUTGERS - YOUNG, Kordell 3 yd run (ITO, Jeremy kick), 5-28 2:32, RUTGERS 34 - NAVY 0

Stats:

	RUTGERS	NAVY
FIRST DOWNS	14	9
RUSHES-YARDS (NET)	33-124	50-113
PASSING YDS (NET)	215	48
Passes Att-Comp-Int	26-15-1	16-4-0
TOTAL OFFENSE PLAYS-YARDS	59-339	66-161
Fumble Returns-Yards	1-7	0-0
Punt Returns-Yards	4-52	1-13
Kickoff Returns-Yards	0-0	2-33
Interception Returns-Yards	0-0	1-10
Punts (Number-Avg)	4-42.2	11-31.6
Fumbles-Lost	2-2	3-1
Penalties-Yards	2-25	6-50
Possession Time	27:40	32:20
Third-Down Conversions	6 of 13	4 of 19
Fourth-Down Conversions	1 of 1	1 of 3
Red-Zone Scores-Chances	4-4	0-0
Sacks By: Number-Yards	7-34	1-13

RUSHING: Rutgers-RICE, Ray 21-93; YOUNG, Kordell 3-28; LEONARD, Brian 4-18; TEAM 2-minus 6; TEEL, Mike 3-minus 9. Navy-Campbell,Reggie 9-44; Ballard, Adam 6-23; Caldwell,Rob 1-20; Kaheaku-Enhada,Kaipo 22-11; Bryant,Jarod 3-5; Singleton, Zerbin 2-5; Kettani,Eric 1-4; Hampton,Brian 6-1.

PASSING: Rutgers-TEEL, Mike 15-26-1-215. Navy-Bryant, Jarod 2-10-0-20; Kaheaku-Enhada,Kaipo 2-6-0-28

RECEIVING: Rutgers-HARRIS, Clark 5-63; UNDERWOOD, Tiqu 4-64; TOWNSEND, James 3-63; LEONARD, Brian 2-18; FOSTER, Willie 1-7. Navy-Tomlinson, Jason 2-28; Singleton, Zerbin 1-22; Campbell, Reggie 1-minus 2.

INTERCEPTIONS: Rutgers-None. Navy-McGown, Jeremy 1-10.

FUMBLES: Rutgers-BECKFORD, Will 1-1; RICE, Ray 1-1. Navy-Kaheaku-Enhada,Kaipo 2-0; Hampton,Brian 1-1.

SACKS (UA-A): Rutgers-MEEKINS, Ramel 2-0; BECKFORD, Will 2-0; JOHNSON,George 0-1; LEE, Glen 0-1; STUDIVANT, Vant 0-1; RENKART, Brando 0-1; FOSTER, Eric 1-0. Navy-Mahoney,David 1-0.

TACKLES (UA-A): Rutgers-MEEKINS, Ramel 4-8; GIRAULT, Ron 1-10; THOMPSON, Devra 2-7; BECKFORD, Will 5-3; FRIERSON, Quint 2-6; FOSTER, Eric 3-3; GREENE, Courtne 2-2; JOHNSON, George 1-3; RENKART, Brando 1-3; LEE, Glen 2-1; STUDIVANT, Vant 0-3; FOSTER, Willie 1-1; COLLINS, Manny 1-1; McCOURTY, Jason 0-2; GIACOBBE, Joe 0-2; KITCHEN, Zaire 1-0; WESTERMAN, Jama 1-0; WOOD, Brandon 1-0; CAMPBELL, Denni 0-1; UNDERWOOD, Tiqu 0-1; WATTS, Gary 0-1. Navy-Miles, Jeromy 5-3; Caldwell, Rob 5-2; Spencer, Irv 5-2; Mahoney, David 5-1; Tidwell,Tyler 2-2; Buffin,Ketric 1-3; Little,Keenan 2-1; McGown, Jeremy 2-1; Wright, David 1-2; Deliz, Jeff 1-0; Chan, John 1-0; Sovie, Clint 0-1; Cylc, Joe 0-1; Adams, Tye 0-1.

Stadium: Navy-Marine Corps MS **Attendance:** 36,918
Kickoff time: 1:37 PM **End of Game:** 4:37 PM **Total elapsed time:** 3:00
Officials: Referee: Gerard McGinn; Umpire: Michael Semches; Linesman: Matthew Fitzger; Line judge: Tod Reese; Back judge: Ronald Boyd; Field judge: James Smith; Side judge: Patrick Garvey; Scorer: Chris Forman
Temperature: 58 F **Wind:** SW 12 mph **Weather:** Sunny

■ **Above Left:** Rutgers defensive lineman Ramel Meekins (60) knocks Navy back-up quarterback Jarod Bryant to the ground. *FRANK H. CONLON*

■ **Left:** Rutgers fans celebrate a touchdown. *FRANK H. CONLON PHOTO*

Rice and Easy

Running back's 225 yards boost RU to 7-0

By TOM LUICCI
STAR-LEDGER STAFF

PITTSBURGH — Any more skeptics?

Any more doubts that Rutgers tailback Ray Rice is a legitimate Heisman Trophy candidate or that the Knights' defense, ranked No. 1 nationally, is for real?

Even the most resolute non-believers had to be convinced after Rutgers' 20-10 Big East victory over Pittsburgh at Heinz Field, when the latest serving of Rice and another stellar defensive effort extended Rutgers' best start in 30 years to 7-0.

"The past three games on the road, all we heard when we came into the stadiums were people chanting 'over-rated, over-rated,'" defensive tackle Eric Foster said. "I don't think we'll be hearing that any more."

The reasons are two-fold: Rice is turning the spectacular into the routine and the defense is simply a dominant unit.

Rice rushed for career highs of 225 yards on 39 carries and completely changed the tenor of the game early in the fourth quarter with one run when Pittsburgh seemed energized after drawing within 13-10.

The Knights were forced set up shop at their 10 with 13:13 to play after that score and seemed to be reeling.

Then, suddenly, they weren't.

Rice took a toss from quarterback Mike Teel and raced 63 yards to get the Knights out of trouble. He ended the 90-yard drive (he rushed for 85 yards on it) with a 1-yard touchdown run with 11:13 to play to push the lead to 10 points.

"The whole stadium got quiet after Ray's run," said Rutgers offensive guard Mike Fladell. "That was just what we needed."

Rutgers coach Greg Schiano called it an "answer-the-bell type run."

The defense did the rest, limiting the Panthers to 67 yards rushing and 169 through the air while putting the breaks on a high-scoring Panthers offense that had gone for 45 points or more three of the past four games.

"That (63-yard run) was a big play, but it was only one play," said Rice, who topped 200 yards rushing for a school-record fourth time in his 19-game career. "The defense played well the whole game. They were amazing. We needed them to keep us close until the offense got untracked and they did that."

■ Far Right: Running back Ray Rice (27) is congratulated by Brian Leonard (23) and a coach after Rice rushed for 225 yards.
FRANK H. CONLON PHOTO

Pitt quarterback Tyler Palko, who entered the game as the national leader in passing efficiency, exited looking quite ordinary. He was 16-of-26 for 169 yards and was sacked five times. The lefty was also limited to 5 rushing yards on 11 attempts.

"He's a good player — a great player," said RU defensive end William Beckford. "We wanted to keep him off-balance and not let him get into a rhythm. You can't let a guy like that get comfortable."

Rutgers harried Palko all night by bringing pressure from everywhere — and every angle.

"Relentless," said Foster. "That's what our defense was. We knew we had to be with Palko."

For the second straight year, Rutgers shut out Pitt in the first half, except this time the Knights only had a 6-0 lead at the break thanks to a couple of Jeremy Ito field goals (compared to 27-0 last year).

Pitt (6-2 overall, 2-1 Big East) cut that to 6-3 on a 46-yard Conor Lee field goal to open the third quarter before Rutgers' offense finally got going. Teel directed a 72-yard drive that ended with his 7-yard pass to Tiquan Underwood just 18 seconds before the end of the third quarter.

Rutgers, with the way its defense was

■ **Far left:** Ray Rice breaks away for a 63-yard run in the fourth quarter. *NOAH K. MURRAY PHOTO*

■ **Below:** Brian Leonard finds a hole to run between a trio of Pittsburgh defenders during the game. *FRANK H. CONLON PHOTO*

playing, looked comfortably in control at 13-3 then.

But Palko answered with his only good drive of the game to open the fourth quarter, capping it with a 10-yard touchdown pass to Oderick Turner, the son of former Giants wide receiver Odessa Turner. It was 13-10 then and the momentum had suddenly shifted.

"Ray got everyone quiet in a hurry, didn't he?" Rutgers running back Brian Leonard said.

The Knights, 2-0 in Big East play for the first time, head home for a Sunday night game against Connecticut after winning three straight road games — all over teams with just one loss at the time.

"Everyone said this was a big test. But we passed it. So, I guess the next one will be a big test," Rice said. "But I think more people outside of this locker room are starting to believe now." ∎

■ **Above:** Pittsburgh quarterback Tyler Palko is sacked by Eric Foster in the first quarter. Foster had two sacks on the day. *NOAH K. MURRAY PHOTO*

■ **Right:** Ray Rice runs for an 8-yard gain in the first quarter. *NOAH K. MURRAY PHOTO*

Left: Mike Teel motions to his receivers while under center during the game. *FRANK H. CONLON PHOTO*

Below: Jeremy Ito congratulates his line as he walks off of the field after making a 32-yard field goal in the first quarter. *NOAH K. MURRAY PHOTO*

■ **Above:** Tight end Clark Harris straight arms Pittsburgh defender Brian Bennett during the game. Harris had three catches during the game. *FRANK H. CONLON PHOTO*

■ **Far right:** Pittsburgh quarterback Tyler Palko (3) scrambles away from a diving Eric Foster. *FRANK H. CONLON PHOTO*

■ **Right:** Rutgers defensive end William Beckford talks to a teammate on the bench late in the game. *FRANK H. CONLON PHOTO*

Left: Fans Ken Miller and Ray Conley cheer for the Scarlet Knights as they take the field before the start of the game. *NOAH K. MURRAY PHOTO*

Far left: Offensive lineman Jeremy Zuttah provides pass protection for quarterback Mike Teel as he moves to block Joe Clermond of Pittsburgh.

FRANK H. CONLON PHOTO

#19 Rutgers vs Pittsburgh

Oct. 21, 2006, at Pittsburgh, PA

Score by Quarters	1	2	3	4	Score	
Rutgers	3	3	7	7	20	Record: (7-0,2-0)
PITT	0	0	3	7	10	Record: (6-2,2-1)

Scoring Summary:

1st 01:28 RUTGERS - ITO, Jeremy 32 yd field goal, 6-23 2:57, RUTGERS 3 - PITT 0
2nd 00:29 RUTGERS - ITO, Jeremy 21 yd field goal, 13-57 3:56, RUTGERS 6 - PITT 0
3rd 10:59 PITT - LEE,Conor 46 yd field goal, 8-37 4:01, RUTGERS 6 - PITT 3
    00:18 RUTGERS - UNDERWOOD, Tiqu 7 yd pass from TEEL, Mike (ITO, Jeremy kick), 9-72 4:23, RUTGERS 13 - PITT 3
4th 13:23 PITT - TURNER,Oderick 8 yd pass from PALKO,Tyler (LEE,Conor kick), 6-65 1:55, RUTGERS 13 - PITT 10
    11:13 RUTGERS - RICE, Ray 1 yd run (ITO, Jeremy kick), 4-90 2:10, RUTGERS 20 - PITT 10

Stats:

	RUTGERS	PITT
FIRST DOWNS	17	12
RUSHES-YARDS (NET)	48-268	26-67
PASSING YDS (NET)	72	169
Passes Att-Comp-Int	18-10-0	26-16-0
TOTAL OFFENSE PLAYS-YARDS	66-340	52-236
Fumble Returns-Yards	0-0	0-0
Punt Returns-Yards	3-23	1-15
Kickoff Returns-Yards	2-50	4-95
Interception Returns-Yards	0-0	0-0
Punts (Number-Avg)	5-45.0	6-43.0
Fumbles-Lost	2-0	2-1
Penalties-Yards	2-15	8-53
Possession Time	34:27	25:33
Third-Down Conversions	7 of 16	5 of 13
Fourth-Down Conversions	0 of 1	0 of 1
Red-Zone Scores-Chances	4-4	1-1
Sacks By: Number-Yards	5-48	0-0

RUSHING: Rutgers-RICE, Ray 39-225; LEONARD, Brian 8-42; YOUNG, Kordell1-1. PITT-STEPHENS-HOWLING, L. 12-55; COLLINS, C. 3-7; PALKO, Tyler 11-5.

PASSING: Rutgers-TEEL, Mike 10-18-0-72. PITT-PALKO, Tyler 16-26-0-169.

RECEIVING: Rutgers-UNDERWOOD, Tiqu 5-41; HARRIS, Clark 3-30; LEONARD, Brian 2-1. PITT-KINDER,Derek 6-70; TURNER,Oderick 3-25; STEPHENS-HOWLING,L. 2-26; BUCHES,Steve 2-23; STRONG,Darrell 1-18; PESTANO,Marcel 1-9; COLLINS,C. 1-minus 2.

INTERCEPTIONS: Rutgers-None. PITT-None.

FUMBLES: Rutgers-FOSTER, Willie 1-0; RICE, Ray 1-0. PITT-KINDER, Derek 1-1; PALKO, Tyler 1-0.

SACKS (UA-A): Rutgers-RENKART, Brando 2-0; FOSTER, Eric 2-0; WESTERMAN, Jama 1-0. PITT-None.

TACKLES (UA-A): Rutgers-McCourty, Devin 6-0; THOMPSON, Devra 5-0;GIRAULT, Ron 4-1; COLLINS, Manny 4-0; GREENE, Courtne 3-1; McCOURTY, Jason 3-0; FOSTER, Eric 3-0; BECKFORD, Will 2-0; RENKART, Brando 2-0; LEWIS, Chenry 2-0; FRIERSON, Quint 1-1; WOOD, Brandon 1-0; PORTER, Joe 1-0; JOHNSON, George 1-0; MEEKINS, Ramel 1-0; WESTERMAN, Jama 1-0; BINES, Blair 1-0; GIACOBBE, Joe 0-1. PITT-BLADES,H.B. 13-6; SESSION,Clint 9-1; McKILLOP,Chris 5-1; CLERMOND,Joe 5-0; BENNETT,Brian 3-1; REVIS,Darrelle 3-0; BRYANT,Sam 2-1; DUNCAN,RASHAAD 2-1; DAVIS,Corey 0-3; CAMPBELL,Tommie 2-0; MUSTAKAS,Gus 0-2; GRAESSLE,Adam 1-0; BUCHES,Steve 1-0; MURRAY,Shane 1-0; PHILLIPS,Mike 1-0; COX,Kennard 1-0.

Stadium: Heinz Field   **Attendance:** 49,620
Kickoff time: 5:47 PM   **End of Game:** 8:57 PM   **Total elapsed time:** 3:10
Officials: Referee: McDaid, John; Umpire: Brenner, Greg; Linesman: Gray, Troy; Line judge: Campbell, Hugh; Back judge: Washington, K.; Field judge: Sokolowski, R.; Side judge: Platt, Bryan; Scorer: Fetchet, John
Temperature: 54 F   **Wind:** W 3 mph   **Weather:** Partly Cloudy

■ **Left:** Head coach Greg Schiano joins his players to celebrate their victory over Pittsburgh. *FRANK H. CONLON PHOTO*

Big plays by defense, special teams help Knights stay perfect

By **TOM LUICCI**
STAR-LEDGER STAFF

The secret is obviously out on Rutgers: Gear up to slow down running back Ray Rice and make quarterback Mike Teel beat you with his arm.

That gameplan, and the dazzling running of former Red Bank Catholic standout Donald Brown II, nearly gave Connecticut a season-saving upset over the 15th-ranked Knights.

But there's a reason this Rutgers team is 8-0 for the first time in 30 years: The Knights have plenty of other ways to beat teams.

That was the case again as Rutgers used an early defensive touchdown and a late special teams score for a 24-13 victory over the Huskies before a crowd of 41,077 at Rutgers Stadium.

The Knights are 3-0 in Big East play for the first time and have an eight-win season for the first time since 1979.

Held without an offensive touchdown in the second half, Rutgers overcame that when Jamal Westerman blocked Chris Pavasaris' punt into the end zone, where teammate Quintero Frierson fell on it for a touchdown with 8:36 to play. That pushed the Knights' lead from 17-13 to 24-13. It marked the second time this year that Rutgers has scored on offense, defense and special teams in a game.

It was all needed too as the Huskies defense kept Rice (79 yards on 22 carries) in check and befuddled Teel and the offense in nearly rallying from a 17-0 halftime deficit.

Brown, a redshirt freshman from Atlantic Highlands, had almost single-handedly carried the Huskies back into the game with 199 rushing yards. He started the second half with a 65-yard touchdown run — the longest against Rutgers' defense this year — to get UConn within 17-7. Then he capped a late third-quarter drive with a 5-yard scoring run.

A botched extra point had UConn (3-5 overall, 0-2 Big East) trailing 17-13 then.

With Connecticut loading the box defensively from the outset with anywhere from seven to nine players, daring Rutgers to throw, Teel and the offense were initially able to respond with a sharp seven-play, 59-yard drive the first time the offense had the ball.

Teel, held to 72 passing yards against Pittsburgh the previous week, was 4-for-4 for 51 yards during the Knights' opening drive, with Rice putting the finishing touches on it with a 5-yard run for a 7-0 lead after just 4:22 had elapsed.

It was Rice's 13th rushing touchdown this season, eight shy of J.J. Jennings' school record set in 1973. Rice still has four regular-season games and a bowl to reach that mark.

But that was the offensive highlight for the

■ **Far left:** Connecticut punter Chris Pavasaris has his fourth-quarter kick blocked by defensive lineman Jamaal Westerman. The kick was recovered in the end zone for a touchdown by Quintero Frierson making the score 24-13.

CHRIS FAYTOK PHOTO

Knights in the half.

As has been the case most of the season, however, it didn't matter because the defense came to the rescue.

Quarterback D.J. Hernandez, who earned the start over Matt Bonislawski, was trying to elude pressure from Rutgers defensive end Jamal Westerman early in the second quarter when he was stripped of the football deep in Connecticut territory, setting off a wild scramble.

Middle linebacker Devraun Thompson originally tried scooping up the ball but couldn't, with Manny Collins finally getting the handle on it at the Huskies' 11-yard line.

Collins, practically carried into the end zone from there by teammate Ramel Meekins, wound up scoring Rutgers' third defensive touchdown of the year to push the Knights' lead to 14-0.

But the Knights' offense kept spinning its wheels, failing to take advantage of excellent field position two other times

■ Far left: During a 22-yard catch and run, on the opening drive, Brian Leonard leaps over Connecticut's Tyvon Branch. The drive finished on the next play with a Ray Rice touchdown. *CHRIS FAYTOK PHOTO*

■ Below: Rutgers fans show their support for the Scarlet Knights. *TIM FARRELL PHOTO*

before the half would end.

On the first, Rutgers had a first-and-10 at the UConn 37 but could only reach the 34 — where place-kicker Jeremy Ito bailed out the Knights with a 51-yard field goal to push the lead to 17-0.

Then just before the half, after Devin McCourty recovered a Hernandez fumble at the UConn 47, Rutgers had 1:25 and all three timeouts to work with for a possible score. But the drive ended after two plays when Teel was intercepted by Tyvon Branch.

Rice, struggling to eke out yard-age against the Huskies' run-stopping defensive strategy, finished the first half with 61 yards on 12 carries.

Teel, meanwhile, was 9-of-14 for 99 yards in the first half.

UConn's best scoring chance in the opening half ended with a missed 51-yard field-goal try by Matt Nuzie late in the first quarter, but the Huskies kept hinting at more because of the running of Brown.

Filling in for the injured Terry Caulley (ankle), Brown had 94 first-half yards (of UConn's 119 then) on 11 carries. ■

■ **Far left:** The Rutgers offensive lineman look to run block on a play as Mike Teel prepares to hand-off the ball during first half action. *CHRIS FAYTOK PHOTO*

■ **Below:** Connecticut running back Donald Brown II, a New Jersey native, scores a touchdown on a 7-yard run in the third quarter. Brown ran for 199 yards on the day. *ANDREW MILLS PHOTO*

■ **Right:** Jeremy Ito pumps his fist after kicking a 51-yard field goal in the second quarter. *TIM FARRELL PHOTO*

■ **Relow right:** Greg Schiano talks to Mike Teel in the first half. Teel went 11-of-24 for 123 yards. *ANDREW MILLS PHOTO*

■ **Below:** Rutgers Jamaal Westerman (90) sacks Connecticut quarterback D. J. Hernandez causing a fumble in the second quarter. Rutgers picked up the ball and ran it in for a score. *TIM FARRELL PHOTO*

■ **Above:** Quarterback Mike Teel gets advice from head coach Greg Schiano in the first half. *ANDREW MILLS PHOTO*

■ **Right:** Rutgers on the bench during the game.

ANDREW MILLS PHOTO

Right: An 'RU' carved pumpkin sits on a table near Mickey Wrublevski, of South Plainfield (right), a 20-year tailgating veteran, before the game. *CHRIS FAYTOK PHOTO*

Far right: A Rutgers fan holds up a sign supporting Ray Rice for the Heisman during the game. Although only running for 79 yards against Connecticut, Rice's season total topped 1,200 yards after the game. *ANDREW MILLS PHOTO*

Below: Ray Rice is mobbed by the student body as he comes off the field after Rutgers defeated Connecticut. *ANDREW MILLS PHOTO*

Connecticut vs #15 Rutgers

Oct. 29, 2006, at Piscataway, NJ

Score by Quarters	1	2	3	4	Score	
Connecticut	0	0	13	0	13	Record: (3-5,0-3)
Rutgers	7	10	0	7	24	Record: (8-0,3-0)

Scoring Summary:

1st 10:38 RUTGERS - RICE, Ray 5 yd run (ITO, Jeremy kick), 7-59 4:22, UCONN 0 - RUTGERS 7

2nd 13:19 RUTGERS - COLLINS, Manny 11 yd fumble recovery (ITO, Jeremy kick), UCONN 0 - RUTGERS 14

08:55 RUTGERS - ITO, Jeremy 51 yd field goal, 6-31 3:02, UCONN 0 - RUTGERS 17

3rd 13:49 UCONN - BROWN, Donald 65 yd run (CIARAVINO, Tony kick), 2-72 1:11, UCONN 7 - RUTGERS 17

00:16 UCONN - BROWN, Donald 7 yd run (BONISLAWSKI, M. rush failed), 8-42 4:34, UCONN 13 - RUTGERS 17

4th 08:36 RUTGERS - FRIERSON, Quint 0 yd blocked punt return (ITO, Jeremy kick), UCONN 13 - RUTGERS 24

Stats:

	UCONN	RUTGERS
FIRST DOWNS	12	11
RUSHES-YARDS (NET)	44-188	29-114
PASSING YDS (NET)	67	123
Passes Att-Comp-Int	17-8-1	24-11-1
TOTAL OFFENSE PLAYS-YARDS	61-255	53-237
Fumble Returns-Yards	0-0	1-11
Punt Returns-Yards	3-44	2-20
Kickoff Returns-Yards	5-103	3-74
Interception Returns-Yards	1-0	1-31
Punts (Number-Avg)	9-34.0	7-43.4
Fumbles-Lost	2-2	1-1
Penalties-Yards	8-52	3-25
Possession Time	33:44	26:16
Third-Down Conversions	3 of 15	3 of 13
Fourth-Down Conversions	0 of 0	1 of 2
Red-Zone Scores-Chances	1-1	1-2
Sacks By: Number-Yards	0-0	6-33

RUSHING: Connecticut-BROWN, Donald 28-199; ANDERSON, Deon 2-4; TEAM 1-minus 4; HERNANDEZ, D.J. 13-minus 11. Rutgers-RICE, Ray 22-79; LEONARD, Brian 7-35.

PASSING: Connecticut-HERNANDEZ, D.J. 8-17-1-67. Rutgers-TEEL, Mike 11-24-1-123.

RECEIVING: Connecticut-ANDERSON, Deon 3-10; MURRAY, Dan 2-23; JEFFERS,Terence 2-21; BROUSE, Steve 1-13. Rutgers-UNDERWOOD, Tiqu 3-38; LEONARD, Brian 3-31; HARRIS, Clark 2-18; BRITT, Kenny 2-13; TOWNSEND, James 1-23.

INTERCEPTIONS: Connecticut-BRANCH, Tyvon 1-0. Rutgers-McCourty, Devin 1-31.

FUMBLES: Connecticut-TEAM 1-1; HERNANDEZ, D.J. 1-1. Rutgers-FOSTER, Willie 1-1.

SACKS (UA-A): Connecticut-None. Rutgers-WESTERMAN, Jama 2-1; BECKFORD, Will 1-0; MEEKINS, Ramel 1-0; RENKART, Brando 1-0; FOSTER, Eric 0-1.

TACKLES (UA-A): Connecticut-BRANCH, Tyvon 4-5; BUTLER, Darius 4-2; DELESTON, Dahna 4-2; HENEGAN, Ryan 2-4; WITTEN, Lindsey 0-6; DAVIS, Dan 1-4; LANSANAH, Danny 2-2; VAUGHN, Robert 1-3; FULLER, Rhema 1-2; MOORE, Donta 1-1; BLAGMAN, Ray 0-2; McCLAIN, Robert 1-0; BRYANT, Aaron 1-0; CULLEN, Desi 1-0; SMITH,Johnathon 0-1. Rutgers-GREENE, Courtne 5-6; FRIERSON, Quint 4-5; McCOURTY, Jason 4-5; WESTERMAN, Jama 4-2; GIRAULT, Ron 2-4; MEEKINS, Ramel 3-2; THOMPSON, Devra 2-3; BECKFORD, Will 2-2; RENKART, Brando 2-2; FOSTER, Eric 1-3; McCourty, Devin 1-2; MALAST, Kevin 1-1; COLLINS, Manny 1-1; LEE, Glen 0-2; JOHNSON, George 0-2; LARYEA, Edmond 1-0; JOHNSON, Sam 1-0; BELJOUR, Jean 1-0; WOOD, Brandon 0-1; LEWIS, Chenry 0-1.

Stadium: Rutgers Stadium   **Attendance:** 41,077
Kickoff time: 8:06 PM   **End of Game:** 11:15 PM   **Total elapsed time:** 3:09
Officials: Officials: Referee: G. McGinn; Umpire: M. Semcheski; Linesman: K. McGrath; Line judge: J. Salmon; Back judge: P. Vargo; Field judge: K. Parham; Side judge: B. Williams; Scorer: RUTGERS
Temperature: 47 F   **Wind:** W 13 mph   **Weather:** Clear

Rutgers shocks Louisville, holds on to remain unbeaten

By **TOM LUICCI**
STAR-LEDGER STAFF

It's okay for Rutgers football fans to spend all day today pinching themselves. Hard as it may be for many of them to believe, this football season isn't a dream.

But it is becoming a dream season.

Sprinkle in a little destiny with lots of Ray Rice and a defense that rates among the nation's best, and what you get is what the biggest game in school history produced last night: Great theater and another Rutgers victory.

Given a second chance thanks to an offsides penalty against Louisville's William Gay, Jeremy Ito took full advantage by making a 28-yard field goal with 13 seconds left to lift 15th-ranked Rutgers to a 28-25 victory over the No. 3-ranked Cardinals before a record crowd of 44,111 at Rutgers Stadium.

It was the first game-winner of Ito's career and came after the junior initially misfired on a 33-yarder with 17 seconds left. Gay's offsides penalty gave Ito, Rutgers' career record-holder with 48 field goals, another chance to be a hero.

Rutgers extended its best start in 30 years to 9-0 and took control of the Big East race at 4-0.

"I was a little spooked on the penalty," Ito said of his first miss. "I saw the guy jump offsides and that distracted me."

The successful second try capped a rally in which the Knights came back from an early 25-7 deficit, setting off a celebration that saw the playing field engulfed by delirious Rutgers fans.

"The atmosphere out there ... you knew it would be (like that), you just didn't know when," Rutgers coach Greg Schiano said. "It was awesome."

"The students were tremendous with the (white Rutgers) towels," said quarterback Mike Teel, who finished 8-of-21 for 189 yards and did just enough with one TD pass. "The Louisville offense had to deal with them coming down on them all game."

Schiano said he wasn't sure right away that Ito had failed on his first attempt at the game-winner.

"I have the worst view on the field. I said, 'Did we miss it?' " he said. "I knew (Gay was offsides). It was right in front of me. So I knew we'd get a second chance."

Rutgers was able to roar back from an 18-point deficit because its defense — ranked in the top five nationally in six categories — completely shut down a Louisville offense ranked No. 2 in the country. The high-octane Cardinals, who dropped to 8-1 overall and 3-1 in the Big East, managed just 53 yards and two first downs while being shut out in the second half.

Rutgers sacked quarterback Brian Brohm five times and held him to a season-low 163 yards

■ Far Right: Fans carry Rutgers kicker Jeremy Ito off the field at the end of the game. Ito's 28-yard kick, with 13 seconds on the clock, won the game for the Scarlet Knights. *CHRIS FAYTOK PHOTO*

Far right: Pam Buxbaum of Toms River hides in the middle of the bushes, waiting to get a photo of the team as they make the "Scarlet Walk" on the way into the stadium before the game. *CHRIS FAYTOK PHOTO*

Below: Rutgers head coach Greg Schiano touches the statue commemorating the first college football game as he leads the team on the "Scarlet Walk" from buses into Rutgers stadium before the game.
CHRIS FAYTOK PHOTO

passing. The Cards, averaging nearly 500 yards of offense per game, finished with 266. "I thought we did a good job of adjusting (in the second half)," said Schiano. "We did some things pressure-wise in the second half (that) takes smart kids. It takes committed kids. It was good."

Rice, meanwhile, rushed for 131 yards and two touchdowns on 22 carries, with his 4-yard run and the ensuing 2-point conversion getting Rutgers within 25-22 late in the third quarter. Ito's 46-yard field goal pulled the Knights even at 25-25 with 10:13 to play.

"It's a tough loss for us," Louisville coach Bobby Petrino said. "I felt like we were in good shape at halftime and we came out in the second half and didn't move the ball offensively. We weren't able to generate anything." The Cardinals had their way for most of the first half in racing to a 25-7 lead that included a 100-yard

kickoff return by JaJuan Spillman.

Rutgers, though, chipped away at that with an 18-yard touchdown run by Rice – set up by a 67-yard pass from Teel to freshman Kenny Britt – to get within 25-14 with 4:59 in the first half.

The second half belonged to the Knights. "We stuck by our motto of 'chop, chop, chop,' " defensive tackle Eric Foster said. "Brohm is a hell of a quarterback, he can expose a defense, but coach Schiano did a great job helping us out the whole game."

Louisville is the highest-rated team Rutgers has ever beaten. ■

■ **Left:** Rutgers receivers gather together in the tunnel leading onto the field before the start of the Rutgers-Louisville Big East football showdown.
ANDREW MILLS PHOTO

■ **Below:** Quarterback Mike Teel fires up teammates before the start of the game.
ANDREW MILLS PHOTO

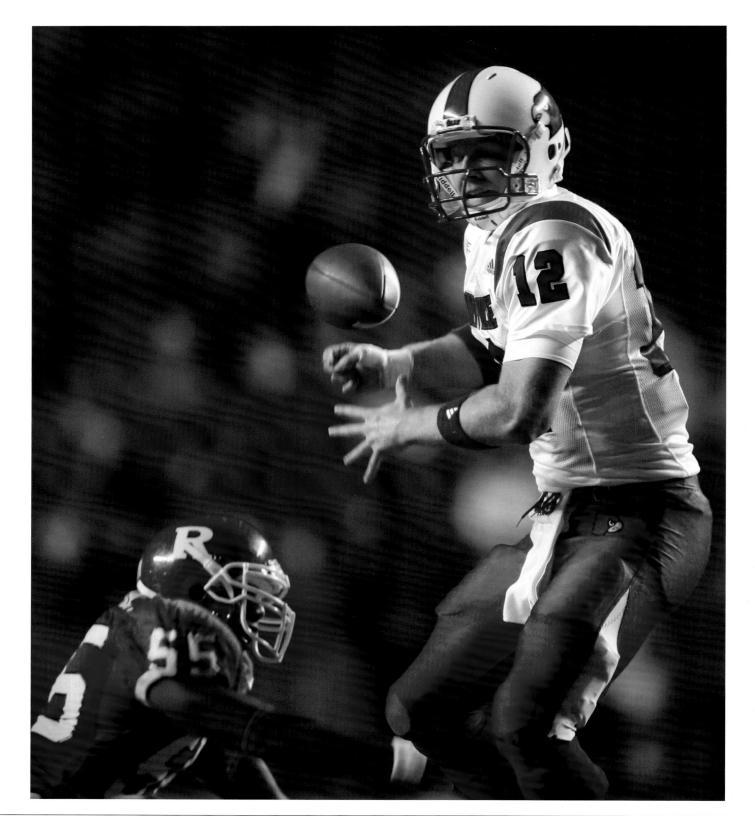

Right: Rutgers linebacker Devraun Thompson causes Louisville quarterback Brian Brohm to fumble during the second quarter.

ANDREW MILLS PHOTO

Far right: A Rutgers fan surfs the crowd after the team scores a touchdown in the first half.

NOAH K. MURRAY PHOTO

■ **Above:** Rutgers receiver Kenny Britt makes a crucial catch in the third quarter. The 67-yard reception left the ball on the Louisville 4-yard line and was followed, on the next play, by a Ray Rice touchdown run. *CHRIS FAYTOK PHOTO*

■ **Left:** Fans in the upper deck of the stadium cheer the Rutgers marching band during the first half. *CHRIS FAYTOK PHOTO*

■ **Above:** Ray Rice falls into the end zone to cap an 82-yard touchdown drive in the third quarter. *NOAH K. MURRAY PHOTO*

■ **Left:** Receiver Dennis Campbell makes a leaping grab for a two-point conversion in the third quarter. The score brought Rutgers to within a field goal of Louisville. *NOAH K. MURRAY PHOTO*

■ **Far left:** Rutgers defensive tackle Eric Foster makes a chopping motion after making a big third-quarter tackle, one of seven he was part of on the night. The chop is one of Greg Schiano's motivational devices. *FRANK H. CONLON PHOTO*

Right: After releasing a pass late in the second half, Louisville quarterback Brian Brohm is clocked by Rutgers linebacker Quintero Frierson. *ANDREW MILLS PHOTO*

Far right: Brian Leonard takes off down the sideline for a 26-yard gain to keep the team's game-winning drive alive. *ANDREW MILLS PHOTO*

Below: Quintero Frierson (50) and Ron Girault (43) take down Louisville wide receiver Mario Urrutia during the second half. The pair were among team leaders in tackles for the game.

CHRIS FAYTOK PHOTO

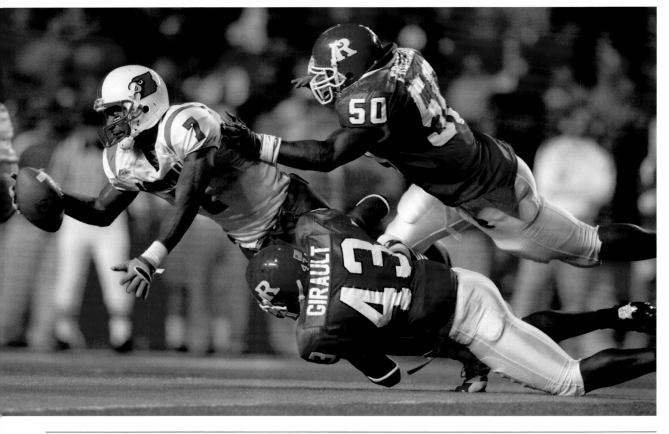

■ **Left:** Rutgers Jeremy Ito celebrates his game winning 28-yard field goal. Ito kicked two fourth-quarter field goals to help bring the team back from what had been a 17-point defecit. *CHRIS FAYTOK PHOTO*

Left: A Rutgers fan hoists a sign celebrating the team's undefeated record as Jeremy Ito kicks the game-winning field goal with 13 seconds to go in the game. *SETH SIDITSKY PHOTO*

Below: A fan leaps from the stands near the end of the game. Thousands rushed the field after the biggest win in Rutgers' long football history. *ANDREW MILLS PHOTO*

■ **Above:** Ramel Meekins, and the photographer, are taken down by the rush of fans as they storm the field after the game. *ANDREW MILLS PHOTO*

■ **Right:** Ashley Goins (center) a freshman sports medicine major, cheers for Rutgers after a big defensive play. *ANDREW MILLS PHOTO*

#3 Louisville vs #15 Rutgers

Nov. 9, 2006, at Piscataway, NJ

Score by Quarters	1	2	3	4	Score	
Louisville	15	10	0	0	25	Record: (8-1,3-1)
Rutgers	7	7	8	6	28	Record: (9-0,4-0)

Scoring Summary:

1st 07:00 LOU - ALLEN, Anthony 2 yd run (CARMODY, Art kick), 8-80 4:59, LOU 7 - RUTGERS 0

04:34 RUTGERS - UNDERWOOD, Tiqu 26 yd pass from TEEL, Mike (ITO, Jeremy kick), 1-26 0:16, LOU 7 - RUTGERS 7

04:17 LOU - SPILLMAN, JaJua 100 yd kickoff return (ALLEN, Anthony rush), LOU 15 - RUTGERS 7

2nd 12:36 LOU - RILEY, Jimmy 5 yd pass from BROHM, Brian (CARMODY, Art kick), 15-61 5:20, LOU 22 - RUTGERS 7

06:34 LOU - CARMODY, Art 39 yd field goal, 8-48 3:57, LOU 25 - RUTGERS 7

04:59 RUTGERS - RICE, Ray 18 yd run (ITO, Jeremy kick), 3-59 1:35, LOU 25 - RUTGERS 14

3rd 04:42 RUTGERS - RICE, Ray 4 yd run (CAMPBELL, Denni pass from TEEL, Mike), 4-82 1:35, LOU 25 - RUTGERS 22

4th 10:13 RUTGERS - ITO, Jeremy 46 yd field goal, 7-33 2:06, LOU 25 - RUTGERS 25

00:13 RUTGERS - ITO, Jeremy 28 yd field goal, 11-80 5:15, LOU 25 - RUTGERS 28

Stats:

	LOUISVILLE	RUTGERS
FIRST DOWNS	13	13
RUSHES-YARDS (NET)	39-103	30-143
PASSING YDS (NET)	163	189
Passes Att-Comp-Int	27-13-1	21-8-1
TOTAL OFFENSE PLAYS-YARDS	66-266	51-332
Fumble Returns-Yards	0-0	0-0
Punt Returns-Yards	4-30	2-16
Kickoff Returns-Yards	5-200	4-58
Interception Returns-Yards	1-0	1-32
Punts (Number-Avg)	7-43.6	6-45.3
Fumbles-Lost	2-0	1-0
Penalties-Yards	8-49	4-35
Possession Time	34:35	25:25
Third-Down Conversions	5 of 17	3 of 11
Fourth-Down Conversions	2 of 2	0 of 0
Red-Zone Scores-Chances	3-3	3-3
Sacks By: Number-Yards	1-5	5-29

RUSHING: Louisville-SMITH, Kolby 19-84; HARRIS, Nate 1-16; ALLEN, Anthony 5-8; BOLEN, Brock 1-0; STRIPLING, Geor 2-minus 1; BROHM, Brian 11-minus 4. Rutgers-RICE, Ray 22-131; LEONARD, Brian 5-21; TEAM 2-minus 4; TEEL, Mike 1-minus 5.

PASSING: Louisville-BROHM, Brian 13-27-1-163. Rutgers-TEEL, Mike 8-21-1-189.

RECEIVING: Louisville-URRUTIA, Mario 5-38; DOUGLAS, Harry 3-97; SMITH, Kolby 3-19; RILEY, Jimmy 2-9. Rutgers-BRITT, Kenny 2-82; YOUNG, Kordell 2-41; UNDERWOOD, Tiqu 2-36; LEONARD, Brian 1-26; RICE, Ray 1-4.

INTERCEPTIONS: Louisville-SMART, Gavin 1-0. Rutgers-THOMPSON, Devra 1-32.

FUMBLES: Louisville-SPILLMAN, JaJua 1-0; BROHM, Brian 1-0. Rutgers-BRITT, Kenny 1-0.

SACKS (UA-A): Louisville-OKOYE, Amobi 1-0. Rutgers-THOMPSON, Devra 2-0; MEEKINS, Ramel 2-0; FOSTER, Eric 0-1; FRIERSON, Quint 0-1.

TACKLES (UA-A): Louisville-SMITH, Preston 3-6; GAY, William 3-3; HARRIS, Nate 1-4; JACKSON, Malik 3-1; SHARP, Brandon 1-3; OKOYE, Amobi 2-1; SMART, Gavin 1-2; MYLES, Lamar 2-0; THOMAS, Lattari 1-1; ALLEN, Anthony 0-2; GRADY, Adrian 0-2; HEYMAN, Earl 1-0; ANDERSON, Zach 1-0; ADAMS, Michael 1-0; FLANNERY, Todd 1-0; BUSSEY, George 0-1; MITCHELL, Mauri 0-1; WOOD, Eric 0-1; GARR, Stephen 0-1; NORTON, Travis 0-1; RUSSELL, Jon 0-1; MATTINGLY, Dane 0-1. Rutgers-THOMPSON, Devra 3-6; FRIERSON, Quint 2-7; MEEKINS, Ramel 5-3; GIRAULT, Ron 4-4; COLLINS, Manny 1-6; FOSTER, Eric 1-6; GREENE, Courtne 2-3; RENKART, Brando 2-2; McCOURTY, Jason 2-2; BECKFORD, Will 1-3; McCourty, Devin 1-3; JOHNSON, George 0-4; KITCHEN, Zaire 2-0; GIACOBBE, Joe 0-2; WOOD, Brandon 1-0; PORTER, Joe 1-0; MUNOZ, Damaso 1-0; LEE, Glen 1-0; CALI, Anthony 0-1.

Stadium: Rutgers Stadium   **Attendance:** 44,111
Kickoff time: 7:48 PM   **End of Game:** 11:05 PM   **Total elapsed time:** 3:17
Officials: Referee: D. Hannigan; Umpire: P. King; Linesman: T. Considine; Line judge: K. Codey; Back judge: R. Boyd; Field judge: R. Street; Side judge: H. Curry; Scorer: RUTGERS
Temperature: 55 F   **Wind:** W 5 mph   **Weather:** Clear

■ **Left:** Ryan Blaszczyk (61) and Dave McClain (75) celebrate on the sidelines near the end of the game. Rutgers won 28-25. *CHRIS FAYTOK PHOTO*

Rutgers hopes of title shot KO'd by Cincinnati

By **TOM LUICCI**
STAR-LEDGER STAFF

CINCINNATI — Maybe the best way to explain what happened to Rutgers is to put it into the Knights' "chop" vernacular.

So here goes: Timber!

Still need a seat on the Rutgers bandwagon? There should be plenty of room now after the way Cincinnati manhandled the No. 7-ranked Knights in a 30-11 upset at Nippert Stadium that dashed any national championship game hopes for coach Greg Schiano's team.

Aided by four Mike Teel interceptions, the Bearcats (6-5) beat the highest-ranked team in school history and did it easily in one of those no-doubt-about-it performances.

"If you play your best and you get beat, you have to say there's nothing more you could have done," Rutgers strong safety Ron Girault said. "But this hurts because we didn't play our best."

Not even close. The reality is, statistically and energy-wise and every other way you want to measure it, this was far and away the worst performance in a season in which Rutgers now stands at 9-1 overall and 4-1, tied with West Virginia and Louisville atop the Big East standings.

So much for the Knights' grandiose plans of working their way into the national championship conversation.

"There's anger and I think they're a little bit stunned," Schiano said of his team's immediate reaction. "Not stunned in a bad way. Stunned in a way (of) 'How did this happen?' It's a good lesson for our program to learn."

The lesson started early, from Jeremy Ito's missed 31-yard field goal on the Knights' second possession to the 10-0 lead

■ Far Right: Wide receiver Kenny Britt on the sidelines after Mike Teel threw an interception in the end zone near the end of the first half.
CHRIS FAYTOK PHOTO

that quarterback Nick Davila, a surprise starter, staked the Bearcats to early in the second quarter when he scrambled 1 yard for a touchdown.

It unraveled for the Knights on their next series.

Facing a third-and-2 from the Cincinnati 21 — and with short-yardage specialist Brian Leonard curiously watching from the sidelines — offensive coordinator Craig Ver Steeg called for a pass.

But Mike Teel found himself pressured by Cincinnati's Adam Hoppel and was forced to roll to his right, where he had to throw while on the run. The badly underthrown pass, apparently intended for James Townsend, was intercepted by DeAngelo Smith and returned 84 yards for a touchdown. Cincinnati had a 17-0 lead then.

And as much as the Bearcats were trying to help Rutgers get back into the game, losing two fumbles inside their 25 in the final 7:39 of the first half, all the Knights could manage was three points from Cincinnati's largesse.

■ **Below:** Rutgers offensive lineman Pedro Sosa goes down with an injury in the first half as members of the Cincinatti defense look on. Sosa returned later in the game. *CHRIS FAYTOK PHOTO*

One reason is because Rutgers threw a 3-yard pass on third-and-6 that forced the Knights to settle for a 34-yard Ito field goal. The other reason is that Teel was intercepted in the end zone by Mike Mickens on a fade to Tiquan Underwood just before the half ended.

It went from bad to worse from there. With tailback Ray Rice (a season-low 54 yards on 18 carries) reduced to the role of spectator as Rutgers tried to play catch-up in the second half, the Knights looked out of synch and lost on offense.

Cincinnati pushed its lead to 20-3, and then to 27-3 when 260-pound tight end Brent Celek took a short pass from Davila and rumbled 83 yards for a touchdown, running over, around and through Rutgers defenders. It eventually grew to 30-3.

"Did we make some mistakes? Yeah, but I don't think we made a ton more mistakes than in games that we won," Schiano said. "What we didn't do was capitalize on opportunities."

Teel finished 21-of-42 for 238 yards with four interceptions and no touchdown passes.

He called the pass that Smith returned for a score "a bad decision."

"I should have taken the sack so we could kick the field goal," he said.

Teel will get plenty of blame for the loss, but the reality is he had more than enough help. Rutgers' nationally-ranked defense was roughed up for 402 yards and a season-high point total. And the unit that came in leading the nation in sacks didn't manage one.

"We had a good week of practice, and usually when that happens we play well," Leonard said. "I don't know how to explain this." ■

■ **Above:** Brian Leonard clutches at his left hamstring as he limps off the field in the first half. Leonard was able to return to the game. *ANDREW MILLS PHOTO*

■ **Left:** Rutgers wide receiver Kenny Britt makes a reception for 5 yards before being forced out of bounds by Cincinnati linebacker Corey Smith in the first half. *ANDREW MILLS PHOTO*

■ **Above:** Quarterback Mike Teel attempts a pass in the first half. *NOAH K. MURRAY PHOTO*

■ **Right:** Running back Kordell Young drops a pass in the first half. *NOAH K. MURRAY PHOTO*

■ **Far right:** Greg Schiano screams from the sidelines during the second half. *CHRIS FAYTOK PHOTO*

■ **Above:** Mike Teel gets hit by Cincinnati defensive end Angelo Craig in the second half. *NOAH K. MURRAY PHOTO*

■ **Above:** Mike Teel walks off of the field after losing to Cincinnati. *NOAH K. MURRAY PHOTO*

■ **Left:** Cincinnati cornerback Mike Mickens intercepts a pass intended for wide receiver Dennis Campbell in the second half. *CHRIS FAYTOK PHOTO*

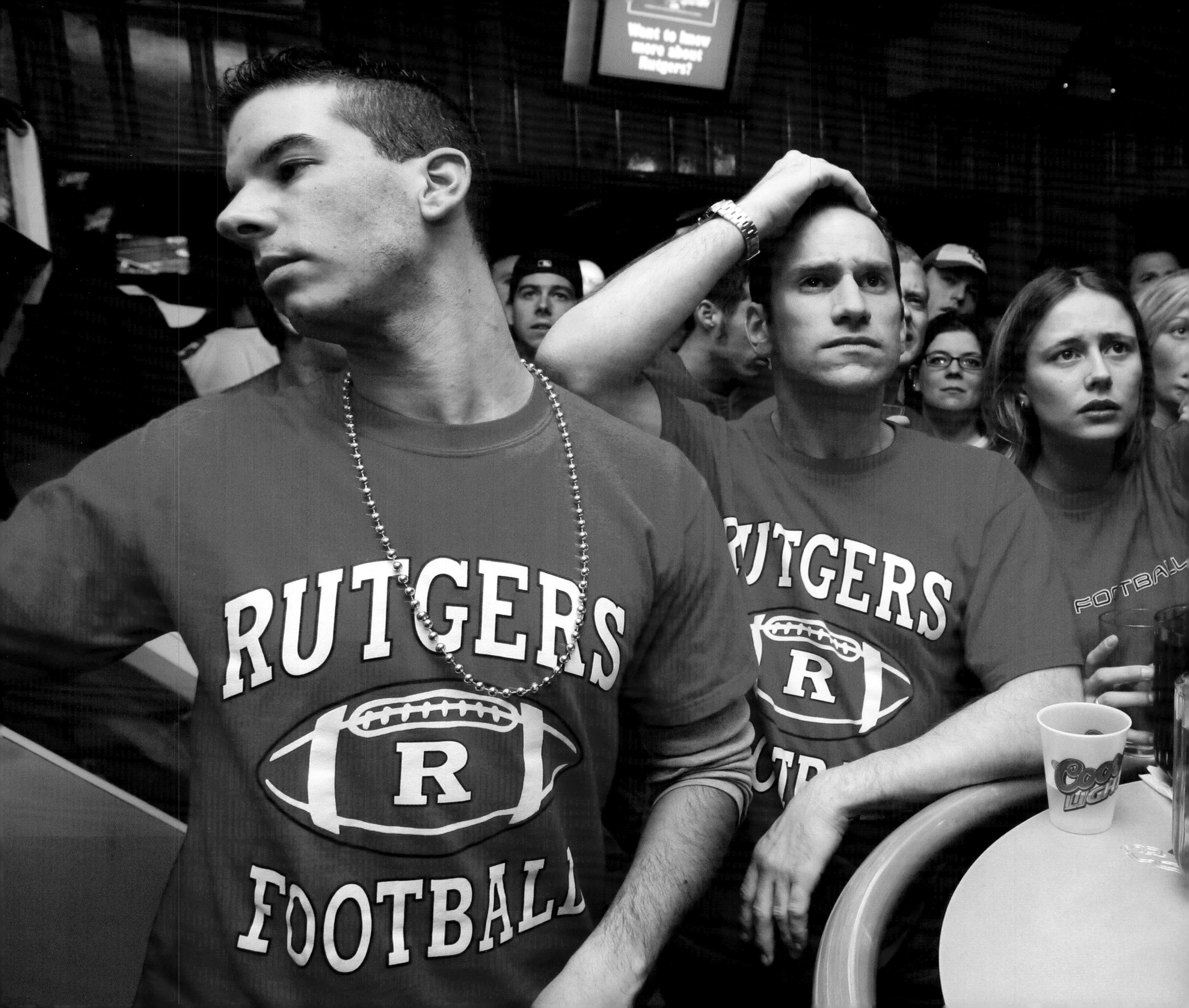
RUTGERS
FOOTBALL

#7 Rutgers vs Cincinnati

Nov. 18, 2006, at Cincinnati, OH

Score by Quarters	1	2	3	4	Score	
Rutgers	0	3	0	8	11	Record: (9-1,4-1)
Cincinnati	3	14	10	3	30	Record: (6-5,3-3)

Scoring Summary:

1st 05:04 CIN- LOVELL, Kevin 32 yd field goal, 11-65 5:34, CIN 3 - RUTGERS 0
2nd 14:16 CIN - DAVILA, Nick 1 yd run (LOVELL, Kevin kick), 10-80 4:08, CIN 10 - RUTGERS 0
09:43 CIN - SMITH, DeAngelo 84 yd interception return (LOVELL, Kevin kick), CIN 17 - RUTGERS 0
05:38 RUTGERS - ITO, Jeremy 34 yd field goal, 4-8 2:01, CIN 17 - RUTGERS 3
3rd 05:35 CIN - LOVELL, Kevin 19 yd field goal, 9-86 5:27, CIN 20 - RUTGERS 3
03:11 CIN - CELEK, Brent 83 yd pass from DAVILA, Nick (LOVELL, Kevin kick), 1-83 0:24, CIN 27 - RUTGERS 3
4th 09:15 CIN - LOVELL, Kevin 27 yd field goal, 16-48 7:31, CIN 30 - RUTGERS 3
05:34 RUTGERS - RICE, Ray 1 yd run (UNDERWOOD, Tiquan pass from TEEL, Mike), 8-63 3:29, CIN 30 - RUTGERS 11

Stats:

	RUTGERS	CIN
FIRST DOWNS	14	15
RUSHES-YARDS (NET)	21-50	46-125
PASSING YDS (NET)	238	277
Passes Att-Comp-Int	42-21-4	15-11-0
TOTAL OFFENSE PLAYS-YARDS	63-288	61-402
Fumble Returns-Yards	0-0	0-0
Punt Returns-Yards	1-11	3-4
Kickoff Returns-Yards	7-136	0-0
Interception Returns-Yards	0-0	4-88
Punts (Number-Avg)	5-40.6	4-38.2
Fumbles-Lost	0-0	3-3
Penalties-Yards	6-45	7-70
Possession Time	27:19	32:41
Third-Down Conversions	7 of 17	6 of 14
Fourth-Down Conversions	1 of 2	1 of 1
Red-Zone Scores-Chances	2-3	4-4
Sacks By: Number-Yards	0-0	1-7

RUSHING: Rutgers-RICE, Ray 18-54; LEONARD, Brian 2-3; TEEL, Mike 1-minus 7. Cincinnati-MOORE, Greg 16-56; GLATTHAAR, Bradley 13-27; DAVILA, Nick 6-23; BENTON, Butler 8-14; JONES, Doug 3-5.

PASSING: Rutgers-TEEL, Mike 21-42-4-238. Cincinnati-DAVILA, Nick 11-15-277.

RECEIVING: Rutgers-HARRIS, Clark 5-102; BRITT, Kenny 9-91; TOWNSEND, James 2-24; LEONARD, Brian 4-13; UNDERWOOD, Tiquan 1-8. Cincinnati-CELEK, Brent 1-83; STEWART, Derrick 2-63; BENTON, Butler 1-62; GOODMAN, Dominick 1-19; ALLI, Kazeem 2-17; BARWIN, Connor 1-9; POLAND, Bill 1-8; MARTIN, Jared 1-8; JONES, Doug 1-8.

INTERCEPTIONS: Rutgers-none. Cincinnati-MICKENS, Mike 2-0; SMITH, DeAngelo 1-84; WILLIAMS, Anthony 1-4.

FUMBLES: Rutgers-none. Cincinnati-HORTON, Antoine 1-1; DAVILA, Nick 1-1; JONES, Doug 1-1.

SACKS (UA-A): Rutgers-none. Cincinnati-BYRD, Terrill 1-0.

TACKLES (UA-A): Rutgers-THOMPSON, Devra, 7-4; MEEKINS, Ramel, 2-8; GIRAULT, Ron, 4-3; McCOURTY, Jason, 4-3; GREENE, Courtne, 5-1; FRIERSON, Quint, 1-5; RENKART, Brando, 3-2; FOSTER, Eric, 1-4; BECKFORD, Will, 2-1; COLLINS, Manny, 2-1; JOHNSON, George, 1-1; WESTERMAN, Jama, 0-2; PORTER, Joe, 1-0; McCOURTY, Devin, 1-0; JOHNSON, Sam, 0-1. Cincinnati-McCULLOUGH, Kevin, 9-1; SMITH, DeAngelo, 5-1; SMITH, Corey, 3-2; WILLIAMS, Anthony, 2-3; ROSS, Dominic, 1-4; NAKAMURA, Haruki, 3-1; MICKENS, Mike, 2-2; HOKE, Anthony, 3-0; MORGAN, Leo, 2-1; WEBSTER, Aaron, 2-0; TOLBERT, Cedric, 0-2; ANDERSON, Trevor, 1-0; BARWIN, Connor, 1-0; BYRD, Terrill, 1-0; SPARKS, Evan, 1-0; DeFILIPPO, Nick, 1-0; CARPENTER, Jon, 0-1; HOPPEL, Adam, 0-1; HORTON, Antoine, 0-1.

Stadium: Nippert Stadium   **Attendance:** 27,804
Kickoff time: 7:45 PM   **End of Game:** 10:58 PM   **Total elapsed time:** 3:13
Officials: Referee: Jeff Maconaghy; Umpire: Greg Brenner; Linesman: Tommy Walsh; Line judge: John Salmon; Back judge: Mark McAnaney; Field judge: Dyrol Prioleau; Side judge: Bryan Platt
Temperature: 47 F   **Wind:** NW 7 mph   **Weather:** Clear

■ **Left:** Rutgers fans Rob DiTondo, Keith Gilman, Julia Kliot and David Goldstein react to a Cincinnati touchdown at the Olive Branch Bar in New Brunswick. *FRANK H. CONLON PHOTO*

Rutgers seeks crowning glory, Rips Syracuse to set up title duel

By TOM LUICCI
STAR-LEDGER STAFF

Greg Schiano immediately put his "24-hour rule" into effect following Rutgers' 38-7 rout of Syracuse at Rutgers Stadium, just as he does after every game. One full day. That's what the players get to dwell on the game they've just played.

This time, the Knights coach needn't have bothered.

Who wants more time to think back — impressive as this performance was — when the most meaningful game in the program's history is the next one?

"I don't need (the 24 hours). I don't think most of the players on this team need it," defensive tackle Eric Foster said. "We're ready to get right to West Virginia."

By manhandling the Orange in the regular-season home finale, a rousing sendoff to a senior class that seemed more like a love-fest between them and a sellout crowd of 43,791, Rutgers put itself in a position that was probably unthinkable back in August.

The 15th-ranked Scarlet Knights will take a 10-1 record into the game at West Virginia, with the Big East title — and the league's accompanying BCS berth — theirs for the taking with a victory. At 5-1 in the league, Rutgers is already assured of its best Big East showing ever.

So, what the Knights are playing for in one game is a trip to, perhaps, the Orange Bowl — or, possibly, the Rose Bowl. Both are still very much in play for Rutgers if it wins the Big East title.

"I'm ready to get started (preparing for) West Virginia right now," sophomore running back Ray Rice said. "I mean right now. This minute. Let's go."

Never mind that West Virginia's loss meant Rutgers could have already clinched the Big East title and a BCS spot if the Knights had not been upset by Cincinnati in their previous game. The important thing, fifth-year senior running back Brian Leonard said, is that "we control our own destiny."

"That's all you can ask for," Leonard said. "It's the last game of the season and we determine what happens to us."

If the Knights can duplicate their performance against hapless Syracuse, which finished 4-8, there's no reason to think they can't become Big East champions.

Rice and Leonard both rushed for over 100 yards, quarterback Mike Teel bounced back from his four-interception performance against the Bearcats in a big way and the defense limited Syracuse to 191 yards.

Leonard rushed for 106 yards and two touchdowns, setting the school scoring record with his second touchdown with eight seconds

■ Far right: Rutgers senior Brian Leonard leads the band in the playing of the Alma Mater after the game.
CHRIS FAYTOK PHOTO

to play — with Schiano keeping his star in the game then just to get the mark at home.

Rice, meanwhile, rushed for 107 yards and a score, while Teel was 10-for-15 for 146 yards with two TD passes (both to emerging star Kenny Britt) and no interceptions.

Those efforts helped Rutgers reach double digits for just the second time in the program's 137-year history. The 11-0 team of 1976, which was represented by 51 players at the game, is the only Rutgers squad to win more than this group.

"To win 10 games anywhere in the country is hard work. Real hard," Schiano said. "To do it at a place that traditionally hasn't been able to is big stuff.

"And to find ourselves in a position to win a Big East championship the final week of the season ... other than myself, I don't know how many thought that would be the case. We've got a real opportunity in front of us. That's where our focus is."

Not even the swirling rumors about Miami's interest in Schiano as its next coach proved to be a distraction for this team.

"I don't pay attention to that. None of us do. That will take you off your focus," Rice said. "We've come too far with too much to play for to lose our focus now."

Schiano reiterated what he has been saying all along during his postgame press conference, saying he "has no plans of going anywhere else."

His team, though, has big plans of going somewhere. Miami, perhaps. Or Pasadena.

"Everything is right there for us," Teel said. "It's up to us now. That's the way you want it to be." ■

■ **Top:** Seniors Brian Leonard, Eric Foster, Ramel Meekins, and Shawn Tucker come out for the coin toss at the beginning of the game. *ANDREW MILLS PHOTO*

■ **Above:** Members of the Rutgers Marching Band perform in the parking lot outside the stadium prior to the game. *ARISTIDE ECONOMOPOULOS PHOTO*

■ **Right:** Willie Foster returns a kickoff for a touchdown in the first quarter. The play was called back though because of a Rutgers penalty. *NOAH K. MURRAY PHOTO*

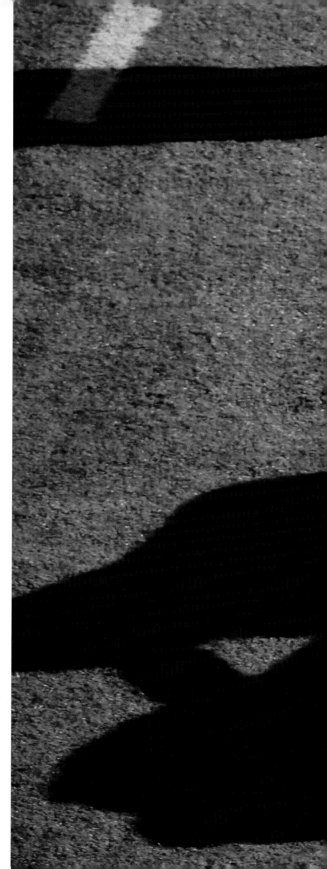

Above: On the hill overlooking the field, Matthew Black, left, watches Keith Soden prepare the cannon for its next discharge after Rutgers scored in the second quarter. They are members of the Middlsex County Militia 2nd Regiment and after Rutgers scores the militia discharges the Centennial Cannon, which was a gift from the class of 1949 during their 20th reunion.

ARISTIDE ECONOMOPOULOS PHOTO

Right: Greg Schiano is dwarfed by offensive lineman Mike Fladell as they talk during the game. *ANDREW MILLS PHOTO*

Far right: Brian Leonard runs away from Syracuse linebacker Jerry Mackey during the first quarter.

CHRIS FAYTOK PHOTO

■ **Above:** The Scarlet Knight mascot cheers with fans along the sideline near the student section. *ARISTIDE ECONOMOPOULOS PHOTO*

■ **Left:** Rutgers sophomore cheerleader Jessica Corcoran watches the game late into the fourth quarter.
ARISTIDE ECONOMOPOULOS PHOTO

■ **Far left:** The Rutgers defense pressures Syracuse deep in Syracuse territory in the second quarter. *ARISTIDE ECONOMOPOULOS PHOTO*

■ **Right:** Brian Leonard, Ray Rice and Greg Schiano celebrate after Leonard scored late in the game. Leonard became Rutgers' career scoring leader with 266 points.

ANDREW MILLS PHOTO

■ **Far right:** Rutgers defensive end Jamaal Westerman goes after Syracuse running back Delone Carter as he gets around a block by Syracuse guard Ryan Durand and Marvin McCall during the second quarter.

CHRIS FAYTOK PHOTO

■ **Below:** Rutgers running back Ray Rice has his helmet knocked off by Syracuse defensive end Cornelius Campbell Jr. and Terrell Lemon during the third quarter.

CHRIS FAYTOK PHOTO

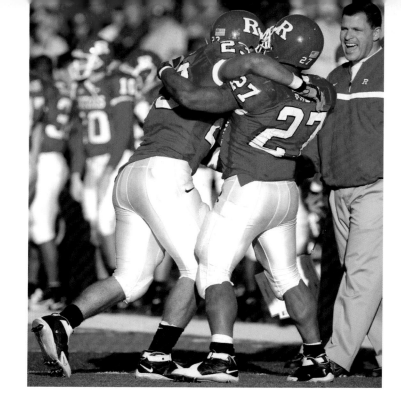

Syracuse vs #15 Rutgers

Nov. 25, 2006, at Piscataway, NJ

Score by Quarters	1	2	3	4	Score	
Syracuse	0	0	0	7	7	Record: (4-8,1-6)
Rutgers	14	7	7	10	38	Record: (10-1,5-1)

Scoring Summary:

1st 09:58 RUTGERS - RICE, Ray 10 yd run (ITO, Jeremy kick), 8-88 5:02, SYRACUSE 0 - RUTGERS 7

06:57 RUTGERS - BRITT, Kenny 38 yd pass from TEEL, Mike (ITO, Jeremy kick), 1-38 0:28, SYRACUSE 0 - RUTGERS 14

2nd 01:17 RUTGERS - BRITT, Kenny 28 yd pass from TEEL, Mike (ITO, Jeremy kick), 7-51 4:14, SYRACUSE 0 - RUTGERS 21

3rd 07:55 RUTGERS - LEONARD, Brian 2 yd run (ITO, Jeremy kick), 9-48 5:06, SYRACUSE 0 - RUTGERS 28

4th 11:49 RUTGERS - ITO, Jeremy 32 yd field goal, 9-51 4:18, SYRACUSE 0 - RUTGERS 31

07:44 SYRACUSE - NESHEIWAT, J. 14 yd pass from ROBINSON, A. (SHADLE, Patrick kick), 10-80 4:05, SYRACUSE 7 - RUTGERS 31

Stats:

	SYRACUSE	RUTGERS
FIRST DOWNS	11	18
RUSHES-YARDS (NET)	31-122	44-217
PASSING YDS (NET)	69	146
Passes Att-Comp-Int	19-10-1	15-10-0
TOTAL OFFENSE PLAYS-YARDS	50-191	59-363
Fumble Returns-Yards	0-0	0-0
Punt Returns-Yards	1-12	0-0
Kickoff Returns-Yards	6-84	2-36
Interception Returns-Yards	0-0	1-26
Punts (Number-Avg)	6-39.2	4-37.0
Fumbles-Lost	1-1	0-0
Penalties-Yards	5-49	4-45
Possession Time	25:17	34:43
Third-Down Conversions	3 of 12	2 of 9
Fourth-Down Conversions	0 of 1	2 of 2
Red-Zone Scores-Chances	1-1	4-4
Sacks By: Number-Yards	0-0	1-4

RUSHING: Syracuse-BRINKLEY, C. 12-51; ROBINSON, A. 5-31; CARTER, Delone 9-25; PATTERSON, P. 4-10; CHIARA, Paul 1-5. Rutgers-RICE, Ray 23-107; LEONARD, Brian 19-106; YOUNG, Kordell 1-2; TEEL, Mike 1-2..

PASSING: Syracuse-PATTERSON, P. 7-16-1-49; ROBINSON, A. 3-3-3-20. Rutgers-TEEL, Mike 10-15-146.

RECEIVING: Syracuse-FERRON, Tom 2-16; MOSS, Rice 2-16; NESHEIWAT, J. 1-14; CHIARA, Paul 2-9; KAPALANGA 1-8; ROBINSON, A. 1-4; CARTER, Delone 1-2. Rutgers-BRITT, Kenny 4-94; LEONARD, Brian 4-27; JOHNSON, Sam 1-23; HARRIS, Clark 1-2.

INTERCEPTIONS: Syracuse-none. Rutgers-GREENE, Courtney 1-26.

FUMBLES: Syracuse-PATTERSON,P. 1-1. Rutgers-None.

SACKS (UA-A): Syracuse-none. Rutgers-McCOURTY, Devin 0-1; FOSTER, Eric 0-1.

TACKLES (UA-A): Syracuse-FIELDS,Joe, 4-6; MACKEY, Jerry, 6-3; SMITH, Kelvin, 6-3; GILBEAUX, B., 5-1; JACKSON, Tanard, 2-3; DAVIS, Dowayne, 0-5; CAMPBELL, C., 2-2; MALJOVEC, Ben, 2-0; LEMON, Terrell, 2-0; McCLAIN, Jameel, 0-2; WILLIAMS, Lee, 0-2; ATKINSON, Jamar, 1-0; OWEN, Mike, 1-0; SANTIAGO, Nick, 1-0; GIRUZZI, V., 1-0; CARTER, Delone, 0-1; CAIN, Luke, 0-1; CHESTNUT, Nick, 0-1; SKLAROSKY, Mike, 0-1; JONES, Arthur, 0-1. Rutgers-FRIERSON, Quint, 3-7; GREENE, Courtney, 5-4; McCourty, Devin, 2-3; THOMPSON, Devra, 2-3; MEEKINS, Ramel, 0-5; GIRAULT, Ron, 3-1; JOHNSON, George, 2-2; WESTERMAN, Jamal, 1-3; RENKART, Brandon, 3-0; FOSTER, Eric, 0-3; WOOD, Brandon, 2-0; ROBERSON, Derri, 1-1; McCOURTY, Jason, 1-0; COLLINS, Manny, 1-0; KITCHEN, Zaire, 1-0; BECKFORD, Will, 0-1; LEWIS, Cherry, 0-1; GIACOBBE, Joe, 0-1; MUNOZ, Damaso, 0-1; MALAST, Kevin, 0-1.

Stadium: Rutgers Stadium   **Attendance:** 43,791
Kickoff time: 12:05 PM   **End of Game:** 2:57 PM   **Total elapsed time:** 2:52
Officials: Officials: Referee: D.Hennigan; Umpire: P.King; Linesman: T.Considine; Line judge: K.Codey; Back judge: G.Dancewicz; Field judge: J.Smith; Side judge: P.Garvey; Scorer: Rutgers
Temperature: 50 F   **Wind:** S 3 mph   **Weather:** Sunny

■ **Left:** Rutgers wide receiver Kenny Britt celebrates his second receiving touchdown with Clark Harris as Syracuse cornerback Tanard Jackson walks away during the first half. *CHRIS FAYTOK PHOTO*

Triple-OT anquish

By **TOM LUICCI**
STAR-LEDGER STAFF

MORGANTOWN, W.Va. — Rutgers' dream season ended in a place that has always been a nightmare for the school.

And as gallant in defeat as the 13th-ranked Knights were, the reality is this: They're now going to the first-year, off-the-national-radar Texas Bowl, not to a prestigious BCS game in January.

West Virginia, which finds a way to torment the Knights during every visit here, did so yet again by dashing Rutgers' Big East title hopes with a 41-39 victory in triple overtime at Mountaineer Field. The Knights' final bid for their first BCS berth ended when cornerback Vaughn Rivers broke up quarterback Mike Teel's 2-point conversion pass to Ray Rice in the end zone.

"They certainly have nothing to be ashamed of," Rutgers coach Greg Schiano said of his team. "They played their hearts out."

The 15th-ranked Mountaineers (10-2) were able to take control for good in the roller-coaster marathon when surprise quarterback starter Jarrett Brown — playing because of a left ankle injury that kept Pat White on the sidelines all game — connected on a 23-yard touchdown pass to Brandon Myles in the third overtime.

Off balance and on the run as he threw, Brown, a redshirt freshman, found Myles a step ahead of cornerback Jason McCourty.

Brown then converted the required 2-point conversion pass to Dorrell Jalloh to give West Virginia a 41-33 lead.

Rutgers, which has defied the odds all season, still had one answer left. It was Rice's 1-yard touchdown run that brought the Knights (10-2) to within 41-39.

NCAA rules require teams to go for the 2-point conversion following touchdowns after the second overtime, but Rutgers' attempt to forge yet another tie — which would have been the fifth of the game — was thwarted by Rivers, dropping the Knights to 0-15 all time in Morgantown.

"Wow. What a ballgame," West Virginia coach Rich Rodriguez said.

The loss spoiled a breakout game for Teel, who was 19-of-26 for 278 yards and a touchdown (with no interceptions).

The teams were tied at 26-26 after the first overtime and at 33-33 after the second one.

Teel, criticized most of the season for ineffective passing, was as good as he could be, especially after West Virginia scored touchdowns on its first two drives of the second half to take a 20-10 lead.

The third-year sophomore quarterback responded to that second score and the 10-point deficit it created with a 72-yard touchdown strike to true freshman Tim Brown on the ensuing series, then drove the Knights 79 yards to create a 20-20 tie on Jeremy Ito's 21-yard field goal with 9:51 to play.

"I just feel bad for the seniors," said Teel. "It's

■ Far right: Brian Leonard walks off the field as Anthony Cali (right) hugs injured teammate Shawn Tucker (center) after Rutgers lost in triple overtime.
ANDREW MILLS PHOTO

one of those situations. You work so hard all season and to come up short is disappointing.

"They made the plays when they had to."

Ito actually had a chance to win the game at the end of regulation, but missed badly on a 52-yard field goal try with 11.5 seconds left.

"I knew I was going to have to hit it perfect," Ito said.

But he was dead-on for a 31-yarder with 3:55 to play that gave the Knights a 23-20 lead — one that could have been bigger if James Townsend hadn't dropped a sure touchdown pass in the end zone one play earlier. That was set up by middle linebacker Devraun Thompson's interception with 7:57 to play.

West Virginia forced overtime on Pat McAfee's 30-yard field with 53 seconds left in regulation.

"It was just a really nice win against a good football team," Rodriguez said.

Brown, making his first career start, was 14-of-29 for 244 yards and one touchdown. He also rushed for 73 yards and a touchdown.

The teams were tied at 26-26 after the first overtime, exchanging field goals then, and were deadlocked at 33-33 after trading touchdowns and extra points in the second overtime.

The West Virginia victory makes Louisville the Big East champ and sends it to a BCS game.

"I'm sure the folks in Louisville are having a real good time now," Rodriguez said. ■

Right: Quarterback Mike Teel fires a pass late in the game. Teel threw for 278 yards in the game. *FRANK H. CONLON PHOTO*

Below: Jeremy Ito reacts after he missed a 52-yard field goal late in the fourth quarter. *ANDREW MILLS PHOTO*

Below right: Rutgers fans Dan Sawyer, left, Lee Musler, right, and Kathleen Fuller, bottom, react to Jeremy Ito's fourth-quarter missed field goal at Olde Queens Tavern in New Brunswick. *SAED HINDASH PHOTO*

Left: Defensive back Ron Girault can't stop West Virginia wide receiver Dorrell Jalloh from making the catch to convert a 2-point conversion during overtime.

CHRIS FAYTOK PHOTO

■ **Above and far right:** Rutgers receiver James Townsend drops what would have been a touchdown pass in the fourth quarter. *ANDREW MILLS PHOTO*

■ **Right:** Mike Teel reacts as James Townsend drops a pass in the end zone in the second half. *CHRIS FAYTOK PHOTO*

#13 Rutgers vs #15 West Virginia
Dec. 2, 2006, at Morgantown, WV

Score by Quarters	1	2	3	4	OT [5 6 7]	Score	
Rutgers	10	0	7	6	16 [3 7 6]	39	Record: (10-2,5-2)
West Virginia	3	3	14	3	18 [3 7 8]	41	Record: (10-2,5-2)

Scoring Summary:

1st 12:50 **RUTGERS**- RICE, Ray 16 yd run (ITO, Jeremy kick), 5-80 2:10, RUTGERS 7 - WVU 0

09:03 **WVU**- MCAFEE, Pat 38 yd field goal, 11-59 3:47, RUTGERS 7 - WVU 3

04:11 **RUTGERS** - ITO, Jeremy 36 yd field goal, 8-61 4:52, RUTGERS 10 - WVU 3

2nd 00:14 **WVU** - MCAFEE, Pat 32 yd field goal, 10-31 1:46, RUTGERS 10 - WVU 6

3rd 10:56 **WVU** - SLATON, Steve 1 yd run (MCAFEE, Pat kick), 7-70 4:04, RUTGERS 10 - WVU 13

05:19 **WVU** - BROWN, Jarrett 40 yd run (MCAFEE, Pat kick), 6-54 2:56, RUTGERS 10 - WVU 20

04:40 **RUTGERS** - BROWN, Tim 72 yd pass from TEEL, Mike (ITO, Jeremy kick), 1-72 0:39, RUTGERS 17 - WVU 20

4th 09:51 **RUTGERS** - ITO, Jeremy 21 yd field goal, 13-79 6:00, RUTGERS 20 - WVU 20

03:55 **RUTGERS** - ITO, Jeremy 31 yd field goal, 8-40 4:02, RUTGERS 23 - WVU 20

00:53 **WVU** - MCAFEE, Pat 30 yd field goal, 11-69 3:02, RUTGERS 23 - WVU 23

OT 15:00 **WVU** - MCAFEE, Pat 42 yd field goal, 4-0 0:00, RUTGERS 23 - WVU 26

15:00 **RUTGERS** - ITO, Jeremy 37 yd field goal, 4-5 0:00, RUTGERS 26 - WVU 26

15:00 **RUTGERS** - LEONARD, Brian 1 yd run (ITO, Jeremy kick), 4-25 0:00, RUTGERS 33 - WVU 26

15:00 **WVU** - SLATON, Steve 1 yd run (MCAFEE, Pat kick), 4-25 0:00, RUTGERS 33 - WVU 33

15:00 **WVU** - MYLES, Brandon 22 yd pass from BROWN, Jarrett (JALLOH, Dorrell pass from BROWN, Jarrett), 2-25 0:00, RUTGERS 33 - WVU 41

15:00 **RUTGERS** - RICE, Ray 1 yd run (TEEL, Mike pass failed), 5-25 0:00, RUTGERS 39 - WVU 41

Stats:

	RUTGERS	WVU
FIRST DOWNS	20	19
RUSHES-YARDS (NET)	37-174	47-195
PASSING YDS (NET)	278	244
Passes Att-Comp-Int	26-19-0	30-14-1
TOTAL OFFENSE PLAYS-YARDS	63-452	77-439
Fumble Returns-Yards	0-0	0-0
Punt Returns-Yards	0-0	2-11
Kickoff Returns-Yards	4-77	6-150
Interception Returns-Yards	1-28	0-0
Punts (Number-Avg)	4-37.8	3-52.7
Fumbles-Lost	1-0	2-0
Penalties-Yards	2-10	6-40
Possession Time	28:18	31:42
Third-Down Conversions	5 of 14	9 of 19
Fourth-Down Conversions	0 of 0	0 of 0
Red-Zone Scores-Chances	7-7	5-5
Sacks By: Number-Yards	2-13	0-0

RUSHING: Rutgers-RICE, Ray 25-129; YOUNG, Kordell 7-39; LEONARD, Brian 4-8; TEAM 1-minus 2. WEST VIRGINIA-SLATON, Steve 23-112; BROWN, Jarrett 17 73; SCHMITT, Owen 4-9; REYNAUD, Darius 1-1; TEAM 1-0; BRUCE, Jeremy 1-0.

PASSING: Rutgers-TEEL, Mike 19-26-0-278. WEST VIRGINIA-BROWN, Jarrett 14-29-1-244; TEAM 0-1-0-0.

RECEIVING: Rutgers-BRITT, Kenny 10-119; UNDERWOOD, Tiqu 3-39; BROWN, Tim 2-90; HARRIS, Clark 2-20; TOWNSEND, James 1-7; LEONARD, Brian 1-3. WEST VIRGINIA-JALLOH, Dorrell 4-92; MYLES, Brandon 4-63; SLATON, Steve 3-37; REYNAUD, Darius 1-26; GONZALES, Tito 1-20; BRUCE, Jeremy 1-6.

INTERCEPTIONS: Rutgers-THOMPSON, Devra 1-28. WEST VIRGINIA-None.

FUMBLES: Rutgers-TEAM 1-0. WEST VIRGINIA-SLATON, Steve 1-0; BROWN, Jarrett 1-0.

SACKS (UA-A): Rutgers-MEEKINS, Ramel 2-0. WEST VIRGINIA-None.

TACKLES (UA-A): Rutgers-THOMPSON, Devra 9-3; GREENE, Courtne 7-4; MEEKINS, Ramel 5-5; RENKART, Brando 3-5; McCOURTY, Jason 4-3; WESTERMAN, Jamal 3-2; FRIERSON, Quint 2-2; GIRAULT, Ron 2-2; BECKFORD, Will 2-1; BELJOUR, Jean 2-1; FOSTER, Eric 1-2; LEE, Glen 2-0; McCourty, Devin 1-0; COLLINS, Manny 1-0; BINES, Blair 1-0; LEWIS, Chenry 0-1; TOWNSEND, James 0-1; JOHNSON, George 0-1; TVERDOV, Peter 0-1. WEST VIRGINIA-HOLMES, John 4-5; MCLEE, Kevin 4-4; ANDREWS, Quinto 4-2; WILLIAMS, Reed 2-4; WICKS, Eric 2-4; YOUNG, Warren 1-5; HENRY, Jay 2-2; RIVERS, Vaughn 2-2; LEWIS, Antonio 3-0; WILSON, Craig 1-2; JONES, Abraham 1-2; DYKES, Keilen 1-2; HATHAWAY, Bobby 1-2; LIEBIG, Pat 1-1; MAGRO, Marc 1-1; WILLIAMS, Larry 0-2; PUGH, Charles 0-2; SHEFFEY, Jeremy 1-0; TATE, Brandon 1-0; ALLEN, Franchot 1-0; DINGLE, Johnny 0-1; IVY, Mortty 0-1.

Stadium: Milan Puskar Stadium   **Attendance:** 60, 299
Kickoff time: 7:45 PM   **End of Game:** 11:37 PM   **Total elapsed time:** 3:52
Officials: Officials: Referee: Gerard McGinn; Umpire: Bruce Palmer; Linesman: Troy Gray; Line judge: Hugh Campbell; Back judge: Mark McAnaney; Field judge: Ben Vasconcells; Side judge: James Brennan
Temperature: 41 F   **Wind:** Calm   **Weather:** Clear

■ Left: Rutgers quarterback Mike Teel and Greg Schiano react after failing to convert the final 2-point conversion during the third overtime. *CHRIS FAYTOK PHOTO*

Rutgers wins first bowl, routs Kansas State

By **TOM LUICCI**
STAR-LEDGER STAFF

HOUSTON — William Beckford was standing off to the side of the field, facing the end zone where several of his teammates had gathered on a makeshift podium to celebrate the first bowl victory in Rutgers history. A fifth-year senior whose first season produced a 1-11 record, the Knights' starting defensive end just wanted to watch the scene.

He wanted to soak it all in as a group that included Brian Leonard, Shawn Tucker, Eric Foster, Ray Rice and Jeremy Zuttah basked in the moment before a sea of raucous fans wearing Rutgers red.

Texas Bowl officials were desperately trying to hand out the game's championship trophy to the group and head coach Greg Schiano, but could barely be heard above the din.

"Being a fifth-year senior, coming in at 1-11 and going through that, you don't realize how important and special a season like this is until you get to the end of it," Beckford said. "I just want to stand here and enjoy it."

The end, he said, was "perfect." Not only to the Knights' magical season, but to his career.

Rutgers manhandled Kansas State in a 37-10 romp before a crowd of 52,210 at Reliant Stadium in the inaugural Texas Bowl, showcasing all of the elements that made the 16th-ranked Knights' season so special.

Dominant defense. Ray Rice's running. And another solid, steady game from quarterback Mike Teel.

It capped an 11-2 season, one that tied a school record for victories.

"This is how it was all year for us," said Zuttah, whose work at right tackle neutralized all-Big 12 defensive end Ian Campbell all game. "It felt like we did whatever we needed to do."

The Knights' 479 yards were a season high, with Rice rushing for 170 yards and one touchdown on 24 carries in earning game MVP honors. Teel balanced that with 268 passing yards (going 16-of-28 with no interceptions), with tight end Clark Harris and true freshman wide receiver Tim Brown both topping 100 yards receiving.

The defense did the rest.

K-State (7-6) was held to 162 yards of offense, with the Wildcats' only touchdown coming on a 76-yard punt return by Yamon Figurs.

■ Far right: Head coach Greg Schiano is doused with water by Willie Foster (84) after Rutgers finished its rout of Kansas State 37-10 in the Texas Bowl.
ANDREW MILLS PHOTO

"It's really a big night, a great night for our program," Schiano said. "To win a bowl game after 137 years of playing the game ... to say we're excited would be an understatement."

Rutgers faced only one challenge all game after jumping out to a 14-0 lead on a pair of Teel touchdown tosses to Brown (four catches for 101 yards).

The Wildcats were able to close within 14-10, with Figurs' punt return providing a spark, before the Knights settled for a 17-10 halftime lead.

But by the opening 3:19 of the second half, the game was essentially over.

Far left: A Rutgers player watches as his teammates participate in the Rodeo Bowl at George Ranch Historical Park as part of Texas Bowl 2006 festivities. Players from Rutgers and Kansas State participated in a number of rodeo style events. *ANDREW MILLS PHOTO*

Left: Rutgers' Aaron Scott and Nikosi Remy try and untie a ribbon from a calf's tail during one of the events in the Rodeo Bowl. *WILLIAM PERLMAN PHOTO*

Below: Rutgers head coach Greg Schiano and the rest of the Rutgers football team got dressed up in cowboy hats and bandanas as part of the Rodeo Bowl. *WILLIAM PERLMAN PHOTO*

Linebacker Quintero Frierson picked off a Josh Freeman pass, returning it 27 yards for a touchdown with Ramel Meekins as an escort, and Rice tacked on a 46-yard touchdown run on Rutgers' next offensive series.

Suddenly, the Knights' lead was 31-10.

"I wasn't worried (at halftime)," said Harris, a fifth-year senior who had seven catches for 122 yards. "They made one great play (on the punt return), but I thought we were in control."

The Knights were.

"Everything came together the way it's supposed to when you have a group of seniors like we have and you want to send them out as winners," Teel said.

"They deserved this. This is about them."

The 25 seniors — nine of them fifth-year guys — couldn't seem to stop smiling as they milled on the field afterward.

"This is one of those feelings you never want to end," said Meekins, a senior. "It's a great feeling."

Meekins was one of the leaders on a defense that forced Freeman, a freshman, into three turnovers (two interceptions and a fumble), sacked him three times and held him to 129 passing yards. K-State rushed for just 31 yards on 21 carries.

"Just watching the older guys enjoy this the way they are now," Teel said on the field in the immediate aftermath of the victory, "makes it all worthwhile." ∎

■ **Far right:** Rutgers players make their way through a sea of red as they walk from buses into Reliant Stadium during festivities before the game. *ANDREW MILLS PHOTO*

■ **Below center:** Kyra Vreeland, 6, of Arlington, TX, Kathy West, of Middletown, NJ (center), and Alek Skarzynski, 9 of Middletown, NJ, cheer for Rutgers as they await the arrival of the team before the game. *CHRIS FAYTOK PHOTO*

■ **Below left:** Rutgers fans did anything they could to get a higher vantage point to see the team arrive at Reliant Stadium before the game. *WILLIAM PERLMAN PHOTO*

■ Far left: Rutgers quarterback Mike Teel runs onto the field with the rest of the team before the start of the Texas Bowl. *CHRIS FAYTOK PHOTO*

■ Left: Wide receiver Tim Brown celebrates with fellow receiver Kenny Britt after Brown's second touchdown catch in the first quarter. *ANDREW MILLS PHOTO*

■ **Left:** Quarterback Mike Teel completes a pass to Clark Harris (81) on the first possession of the game. *ANDREW MILLS PHOTO*

■ **Below:** Wide receiver Tim Brown makes a touchdown reception in front of Kansas State defensive back Justin McKinney in the first half. *CHRIS FAYTOK PHOTO*

Far left: Ray Rice runs for a 46-yard touchdown in the third quarter. Rice was the MVP of the game with 170 yards rushing. *WILLIAM PERLMAN PHOTO*

Left: Rutgers linebackers Devraun Thompson and Ron Girault sack Kansas State quarterback Josh Freeman. *CHRIS FAYTOK PHOTO*

Below : Wide receiver Kenny Britt makes a third-down reception as Kansas State linebacker Brandon Archer lands on his head and linebacker Leroy White makes the tackle in the first half. Rutgers drove down the field and scored on a Jeremy Ito field goal during the series. *CHRIS FAYTOK PHOTO*

Below right: Kenny Britt makes a leaping catch over Kansas State's Joshua Moore in the second quarter. *WILLIAM PERLMAN PHOTO*

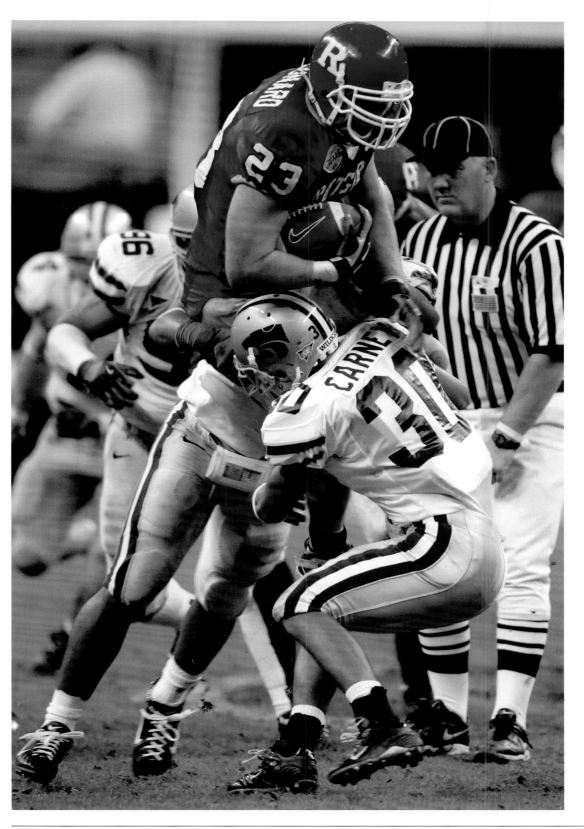

Right: Rutgers defensive lineman Ramel Meekins causes Kansas State quarterback Josh Freeman to fumble in the 4th quarter. Jamaal Westerman (90) recovered the ball for Rutgers. *CHRIS FAYTOK PHOTO*

Left: Greg Schiano is soaked with water as the team runs out onto the field to celebrate the win. *CHRIS FAYTOK PHOTO*

Below: Ray Rice and Brian Leonard shake hands after Rice was named MVP of the game. *WILLIAM PERLMAN PHOTO*

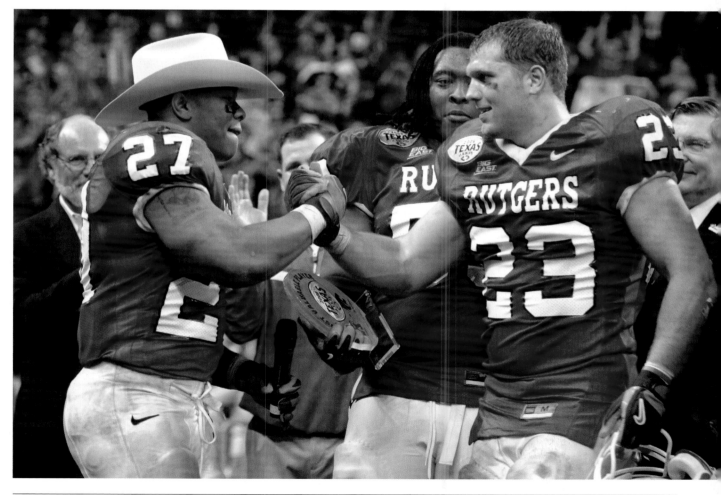

#16 Rutgers vs Kansas State

Dec. 28, 2006, at Houston, TX

Score by Quarters	1	2	3	4	Score	
Rutgers	14	3	14	6	37	Record: (11-2)
Kansas State	0	10	0	0	10	Record: (7-6)

Scoring Summary:

1st 07:12 RUTGERS - BROWN, Tim 14 yd pass from TEEL, Mike (ITO, Jeremy kick), 6-35 2:58, RUTGERS 7 - KSTATE 0

02:42 RUTGERS - BROWN, Tim 49 yd pass from TEEL, Mike (ITO, Jeremy kick), 3-79 1:40, RUTGERS 14 - KSTATE 0

2nd 13:32 KSTATE - Snodgrass, Jeff 44 yd field goal, 9-53 4:10, RUTGERS 14 - KSTATE 3

09:37 KSTATE - Figurs, Yamon 76 yd punt return (Snodgrass, Jeff kick), , RUTGERS 14 - KSTATE 10

00:49 RUTGERS - ITO, Jeremy 37 yd field goal, 10-44 2:30, RUTGERS 17 - KSTATE 10

3rd 14:27 RUTGERS - FRIERSON, Quint 27 yd interception return (ITO, Jeremy kick), RUTGERS 24 - KSTATE 10

11:41 RUTGERS - RICE, Ray 46 yd run (ITO, Jeremy kick), 2-68 0:57, RUTGERS 31 - KSTATE 10

4th 14:51 RUTGERS - ITO, Jeremy 23 yd field goal, 7-16 3:33, RUTGERS 34 - KSTATE 10

08:06 RUTGERS - ITO, Jeremy 21 yd field goal, 8-35 4:25, RUTGERS 37 - KSTATE 10

Stats:

	RUTGERS	KANSAS STATE
FIRST DOWNS	21	6
RUSHES-YARDS (NET)	37-211	21-31
PASSING YDS (NET)	268	131
Passes Att-Comp-Int	28-16-0	24-12-2
TOTAL OFFENSE PLAYS-YARDS	65-479	45-162
Fumble Returns-Yards	0-0	0-0
Punt Returns-Yards	0-0	2-78
Kickoff Returns-Yards	3-81	5-111
Interception Returns-Yards	2-61	0-0
Punts (Number-Avg)	2-42.5	5-42.4
Fumbles-Lost	0-0	1-1
Penalties-Yards	5-30	9-59
Possession Time	36:20	23:40
Third-Down Conversions	6 of 14	1 of 10
Fourth-Down Conversions	0 of 1	1 of 3
Red-Zone Scores-Chances	4-8	0-0
Sacks By: Number-Yards	3-24	0-0

RUSHING: Rutgers-RICE, Ray 24-170; LEONARD, Brian 11-44; TEAM 2-minus 3. Kansas State-Johnson, James 6-20; Patton, Leon 8-14; Anders, Donnie 1-2; Freeman, Josh 6-minus 5.

PASSING: Rutgers-TEEL, Mike 16-28-0-268. Kansas State-Freeman, Josh 10-21-2-129; Meier, Dylan 2-3-0-2.

RECEIVING: Rutgers-HARRIS, Clark 7-122; BROWN, Tim 4-101; BRITT, Kenny 2-41; LEONARD, Brian 2-6; YOUNG, Kordell 1-minus 2. Kansas State-Nelson, Jordy 4-81; Norwood,Rashaad 2-40; Johnson, James 2-0; Gonzalez,Daniel 1-11; Pooschke, Mike 1-7; Patton, Leon 1-1; Meier, Dylan 1-minus 9.

INTERCEPTIONS: Rutgers-GIRAULT, Ron 1-34; FRIERSON, Quint 1-27. Kansas State-None.

FUMBLES: Rutgers-None. Kansas State-Freeman, Josh 1-1.

SACKS (UA-A): Rutgers-WESTERMAN, Jama 2-0; GIRAULT, Ron 1-0. Kansas State-None.

TACKLES (UA-A): Rutgers-GIRAULT, Ron 5-1; McCourty, Devin 5-0; McCOURTY, Jason 5-0; FRIERSON, Quint 2-3; MEEKINS, Ramel 4-0; THOMPSON, Devra 3-0; ROBERSON, Derri 2-1; RENKART, Brando 2-1; WESTERMAN, Jama 2-1; GREENE, Courtne 2-0; COLLINS, Manny 1-0; MALAST, Kevin 1-0; BECKFORD, Will 1-0; PORTER, Joe 1-0; GIACOBBE, Joe 0-1; JOHNSON, George 0-1. Kansas State-Archer, Brandon 4-5; McKinney,Justin 6-1; Moore, Joshua 6-1; Watts, Marcus 4-3; Campbell, Ian 3-4; Diles, Zach 2-5; Jackson, Rob 3-2; Williams, Kyle 4-0; Walker, Reggie 4-0; Erker, Andrew 3-1; Roland, Justin 3-0; Seiler, Blake 2-0; Moore, Antwon 1-1; Perry, Marcus 1-1; Faustin, Vlad 1-0; Moran, Alphonso 1-0; Cline, Steven 1-0; Houlik, John 0-1; Wilson, Cedric 0-1; Carney, Chris 0-1.

Stadium: Reliant Stadium   **Attendance:** 52,210

Kickoff time: 7:12 pm   **End of Game:** 10:29 pm   **Total elapsed time:** 3:17

Officials: Referee: Jeff Flanagan; Umpire: Mike Wooten; Linesman: Tyrone Davis; Line judge: Tommy Giles Jr.; Back judge: Doug Rhoads; Field judge: Chris Brown; Side judge: Timon Oujiri; Scorer: Mark Sanders;

Weather: Indoors-roof closed

■ **Left:** Rutgers players, coach Greg Schiano and University President Richard McCormick sing the Alma Mater after winning the Texas Bowl 37-10. *CHRIS FAYTOK PHOTO*

ACKNOWLEDGMENTS

Editors

Seth Siditsky and Pim Van Hemmen

Design

Brad Fenison, The Pediment Group, Inc.

Copy Editors

Tom Bergeron and Tom Curran

Additional Photo Editors

John Figlar, Dave Hawkins and Steve Miller

Marketing

Robert Provost, Karen Fazio and Carla Lewis

Special thanks also to Michelle Segall, the rest of the photo and sports departments at
The Star-Ledger, the media relations staff at Rutgers, and of course the Rutgers football team.

PHOTOGRAPHY & WRITING

FRANK H. CONLON

Frank Conlon has been a photographer with The Star-Ledger since the early 1990s and has covered Rutgers since graduating from Livingston College in 1985. When not covering assignments for the paper he can be found at his Kingwood Township home working in the barn with with his horses and catching up on his chores.

ARISTIDE ECONOMOPOULOS

Aristide Economopoulos has covered just about everything since he joined the paper in 2000, including the 9/11 attacks in New York City, the 2004 Athens Olympics and the past two presidential elections. And how could we forget: hog wrestling in Indiana.

TIM FARRELL

Tim Farrell has covered a variety of sports since joining the paper in 1994. In the summer, he covers everyone's favorite sport: eating. Farrell serves as the official photographer of the Star-Ledger's Munchmobile.

CHRIS FAYTOK

Chris Faytok shot his first Rutgers game in 1995, a 27-17 loss to Donovan McNabb's Syracuse team. Since then, he has covered three Olympic Games, five World Series, two Stanley Cup Finals, two NBA Finals, a Super Bowl and one Texas Bowl.

SAED HINDASH

Saed Hindash has been with the Star-Ledger since 2000. His work is seen throughout the paper. In 2002, he won the national Dart Award for a story about a Siberian orphan who died tragically.

TOM LUICCI

Tom Luicci has been writing for The Star-Ledger since 1979. A 1977 Rutgers graduate, he chronicled the school's 11-0 football season in 1976 for the student newspaper. After a brief 30-year wait, he finally saw the football program return to prominence.

ANDREW MILLS

Andrew Mills has been at The Star-Ledger since 1996 covering every major sporting event you can name. During the summer, he covers something else — the shore in Manasquan, where he still works as a lifeguard in his hometown.

NOAH K. MURRAY

Noah Murray began his photography career at The Star-Ledger as a lab technician. After a stint as a staff photographer at The Asbury Park Press he returned to The Star-Ledger as a photographer in 2000. He has covered various sporting events including the World Series and the NBA Finals.

WILLIAM PERLMAN

Bill Perlman has been a staff photographer for The Star-Ledger since 1990. He has covered the World Series, NBA Finals, Stanley Cup Finals, the NCAA Tournament and World Cup Soccer. Perlman grew up in East Brunswick.

SETH SIDITSKY

Seth Siditsky has been the sports photo editor at The Star-Ledger since 2003. He coordinates daily sports coverage and oversees major projects — this book being his latest effort.

MITSU YASUKAWA

Mitsu Yasukawa has been a staff photographer at The Star-Ledger since 2000. Prior to joining the paper, he freelanced for various publications and was a staff photographer at New York Newsday and the New York Daily News.

If you would like to contact The Star-Ledger you can reach us at 1 Star-Ledger Plaza, Newark, NJ 07102 or 1-888-STARLEDGER. If you would like to reach the photo department please call 1-973-392-1530.

■ Right: Brian Leonard kisses the Texas Bowl trophy. *CHRIS FAYTOK PHOTO*